GET A LIFE!

SINGLE to *settled*

Elizabeth Clark

Hodder Arnold

A MEMBER OF THE HODDER HEADLINE GROUP

Cover © Comstock Images/Getty Images
Photodisc/Getty Images
Stockbyte/Getty Images

Illustrations by Veronica Palmieri/www.folioart.co.uk
Photographs p12 © Willie Maldonado/Taxi/Getty Images
p40 © Michael Kevin Daly/CORBIS
p89 © Image Source/Rex Features
p96 © Britt Erlanson/ The Image Bank/Getty Images
p119 © Brooke Fasani/CORBIS
p128 © Ellen Stagg/Stone+/Getty Images
p154 © Hummer/Taxi/Getty Images
p161 © Alain Daussin/The Image Bank/Getty Images
p212 © Simon Plant/Iconical/Getty Images

Orders: Please contact Bookpoint Ltd, 130 Milton Park, Abingdon, Oxon OX14 4SB.
Telephone: (44) 01235 827720, Fax: (44) 01235 400454. Lines are open from 9.00 to 18.00, Monday
to Saturday, with a 24-hour message answering service. You can also order through our website
www.hoddereducation.com

British Library Cataloguing in Publication Data
A catalogue record for this title is available from the British Library.

ISBN-10: 0 340 90800 9
ISBN-13: 9 780340 908006

First published   2006
Impression number   10 9 8 7 6 5 4 3 2 1
Year   2008   2007   2006

Typeset by Pantek Arts Ltd, Maidstone, Kent.
Printed in Great Britain for Hodder Arnold, a division of Hodder Headline,
338 Euston Road, London, NW1 3BH, by Bath Press, Bath.

Hodder Headline's policy is to use papers that are natural, renewable and recyclable products and made
from wood grown in sustainable forests. The logging and manufacturing processes are expected to
conform to the environmental regulations of the country of origin.

Every effort has been made to trace copyright for material used in this book. The authors and
publishers would be happy to make arrangements with any holder of copyright whom it has not been
possible to trace successfully by the time of going to press.

CONTENTS

CONTENTS

DEDICATION

I dedicate this book to the three people who make my world go round – my children Calum and Lucy, and my man Glyn, without whose perpetual support and tolerance of lack of pack-lunches, this book would not have been possible.

INTRODUCTION

Hi! I'm Elizabeth Clark, your *Single to Settled* coach. I'd like to welcome you to the programme. Follow the plan and after just 100 days you'll have:

- Chosen or be well on the way to choosing the man of your dreams
- Encountered many potential dates through the 16 different dating avenues
- Boosted your confidence and expanded your comfort zones with some great tips, techniques and exercises
- Enhanced your personal and professional relationships
- Gained self-insight
- Acquired all the information you need to build the foundations of a solid, durable relationship
- Had a great time doing it.

The nature of this book and the timescales involved mean that the emphasis is on you being proactive. You could just sit at home and wait for Mr Right to appear, but that would be a much shorter book – although it would take considerably longer than 100 days.

TOP TIP

- What not to read ... anything you feel isn't relevant.

I'm not asking you to do anything that hasn't been done by myself or by many of my happy course delegates. Being thirty-something, divorced after 11 years of marriage, living in a cultural backwater, with a couple of kids and being self-employed, I've dated all sorts of men, from millionaires to models. If I can settle down with a gorgeous, intelligent, caring man, you can too.

The *Single to Settled* programme is structured into 100 days, although you can feel free to speed up or slow down according to your time and progress. Over this time period I introduce topics, revisit them later and build on them until you're fully familiar with every dimension of the subject matter. I don't expect that every single topic will relate to everybody – pick what is appropriate to you. You may also wish to buy yourself a little notebook and keep a daily diary along the way to mark your progress. You also have the option of receiving daily text messages that will provide you with the extra motivation you need to achieve your goal.

Your comfort zone is going to be stretched, which is a good thing. If your comfort zone isn't stretching, it's shrinking. Therefore it's important, for a confident and positive outlook, to exercise it regularly. Courage grows after we've done the things we fear, not before. Take note of your comfort zones now and see how much bigger they are by the time you're finished. Not only will you have Mr Right on your arm, you'll be ready to take on anything.

Getting a date is only the start. It is also important to understand how the chemical effects of lust and love affect how much effort we have to put into a relationship to make it work. Also vital are dating etiquette and the rules for the foundation of a long-term relationship. This book covers all this and more, and will ensure you keep the Right man for you.

I have various more in-depth factsheets relating to some of the topics in your programme, so feel free to drop me a line for more information. If you have a burning question that I haven't covered, or you want to tell me about your success stories, I'll be delighted to hear from you. E-mail me at settled@rapportunlimited.co.uk

My final piece of advice is to enjoy your programme. If you face it like a chore to be completed that's exactly how it will feel. Be excited about the day's activity, what's coming next and who's going to be around the next corner. Positivity is infectious and attractive. Besides, dating is so much fun – and success is only 100 days away.

TOP TIP

♦ From my experience I can predict that if you give it 100% effort you will succeed.

Daily Text Message Service

 A unique, interactive text messaging service is available★ with this book. Daily texts provide inspiration as well as key tips and advice to help you achieve your goal.

By subscribing at the beginning of a 10-day period you will receive a message each day encouraging you and supporting the guidance already given in the book for that day.

So, what are you waiting for? Text the keyword on Day 1 to 80881 to receive invaluable advice that will help you to achieve your full transformation.

★ UK only

CHAPTER 1

GET READY

Subscribe now to your set of 10 daily text messages. Just text 'Settled 1' to 80881 and receive the advice and encouragement you need to go from *Single* to *Settled*.

Each set of messages costs £1.50. Please see page x for full terms and conditions.

Know what's stopping you

There's always a good reason for doing things – unfortunately, we often find that there are even better reasons for not doing them. Today we will look at the six most common excuses for not making the effort to find a new partner. The chances are that you'll fall into at least one of these broad categories. Let me address these myths and banish these limitations from your expectations.

1 People tell me if I stop looking, I'll find him where I least expect it

There's a chance that you may find your man in an activity other than the ones I'm going to list, but the fact is that if you stop looking, you'll stop seeing and you'll be missing opportunities that are right under your nose. Read more on Day 38.

2 If I could just lose a bit of weight I'd be more confident about meeting someone new

We'd all love to have an hour-glass figure, but unless you can get over the 'diets always begin tomorrow' hurdle, it's going to remain a pipe dream. Next time you're out, have a good look around – is every half of a couple accompanied by a stick-thin woman? No. I don't know of a woman who had this reservation that didn't go on to get herself a man, regardless of her weight. Read Day 10 for some skinny tips.

3 I never get any opportunities to meet anyone new

Every day is an opportunity. It may not feel like it now, but when you've run through all your options you'll start to see opportunities you didn't know existed. I live in an area where bachelors are married off as soon as they hit puberty and all the divorcees hang out in clubs with women half their age. If I can find a man – you certainly can.

4 If I was a bit more confident I'd be out there like a shot

You're going to get one of the best lessons in confidence that money can buy and you've only paid the price of this book for it. By the time you've worked through a few chapters there'll be no stopping you.

5 All the best guys are taken and there's no-one to match my ex

Of course they're not all taken. You're either attracted to the wrong sort of man (the married variety) or you're looking in the wrong places – Chapter 3 will sort this excuse out. Having a rose-tinted view of your ex is hindering your progress – why do you hold this man is such high esteem? There are many men equal to him and better. Look beyond your ex and towards an improved Mr Right.

6 Nobody is interested in women with baggage

You're talking to a mother of two whose remit for a new lover included no children and preferably no parents either. There are some great men out there who will adore your children, you just have to be very selective.

Enough of your excuses, there's absolutely no reason why you can't crack on from where you are now, with the help of *Singled to Settled*, to find exactly what you're looking for.

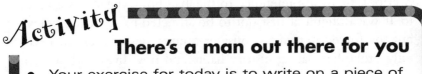

Activity
There's a man out there for you

- Your exercise for today is to write on a piece of paper 'There's a man out there for me and I'm going to find him.' Stick it somewhere prominent (fridge, bathroom mirror, etc.) and read it out – and believe it – every time you see it.

- How do you feel doing this?
  - **Confident**
    Great – your positive affirmations will be working for you in no time.
  - **Silly**
    Don't be – your subconscious doesn't have a sense of humour, it takes everything literally. If you tell it you're going to fail it believes you, if you tell it you're going to succeed, it believes you. Fill it full of positive thoughts and watch your success follow.

GET READY

Learn from your past

Before you think about skipping sections, a word to the wise: if you don't learn from what you've done before and consider what you actually value in a partner you're likely to repeat the same mistakes all over again. You have to live your life forwards but you can only understand it by looking backwards.

CASE STUDY

Anna had a disastrous dating history. Her ex-husband had been unattentive, a smoker and a drinker who mainly worked away from home. When he eventually left to make some other poor woman's life a misery, she decided she wanted a local boyfriend who was a non-smoker and who made her feel special. Despite her best intentions, she spent three years not realising she was dismissing her ideal date prematurely – she couldn't help but overlook them in preference to the 'bad boy' type she was used to. It was difficult at first not to be attracted to what she knew, but she forced herself to consider other types of men, successfully broke her dating history habit, and now lives with a man who adores her.

GET READY

Your dating history

- Learning from the past is essential if you are to prevent yourself from repeating old mistakes. Let's start by taking a look at your dating history. Complete a chart like the one below. Do it now!

Name of partner	Length of relationship	What attracted you to them	Things you hated about them	Who ended it and why

GET READY

Spot your dating habits

It's important to review your dating history so that the way is clear for you to have the best chance of success when meeting and impressing Mr Right. You can't change what has happened in the past but the future is in your power.

You've had a day to mull over the ups and downs of your dating history, did you see any patterns emerging? If 'No' then you can be reassured that you have no persistent relationship habits (at least not yet). If 'Yes'; then read on …

Do you always like/dislike the same qualities in your partners?

If so, this could be a key part to your finding Mr Right. You need to be more open-minded when meeting people. Traits that we recognise allow us to fall straight into our comfort zone, automatically making us feel easier, even if it isn't right for us.

Are all your relationships the same length?

If so, then you could be a serial monogamist. Some people love the buzz a new person gives them. When that feeling goes they assume that they're no longer attracted to their partner (when it may simply be that the relationship needs a bit of effort).

Alternatively, if your relationships are all of a very short length, there could be a number of reasons – these will unfold as you go through the book.

GET READY

TOP TIP

♦ Mother nature gives us all the hormones we need to enjoy the first 12–24 months of a relationship without really having to make an effort. Thereafter you have to resort to your own resources in order to maintain those initial heady levels.

Are you always the dumper or the dumpee?

As the dumpee you may be overstaying your welcome in the relationship, not paying attention to the dissatisfied signs they're giving you, or simply continually picking Mr Wrong.

As the dumper, are you getting in first and dumping before you've been dumped? Are you always walking away at the first sign of trouble? Or are you setting an unrealistically high expectation from your partner?

All these questions will be answered as we progress through the book.

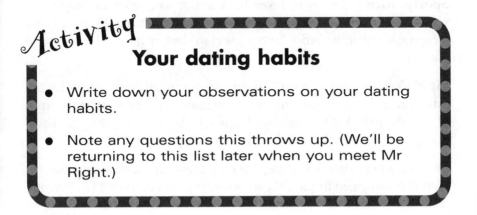

Activity
Your dating habits

● Write down your observations on your dating habits.

● Note any questions this throws up. (We'll be returning to this list later when you meet Mr Right.)

GET READY

What type do you go for?

Your task is to identify which type of man you've dated before. Tomorrow you can cross-check to see who will drive you nuts and who you are more suited to.

CASE STUDY

Anna's new boyfriend was a 'bad boy', not only was he bad for her confidence, he made her paranoid and act out of character. One night Anna found herself on a night out in his home town. She could have sworn she saw him although he had claimed he was away. However, she decided to pay him a visit in the early hours on the way home. Unusually for Anna, she picked up some pebbles and threw them at his upstairs window to no avail. She decided the only thing heavy enough that wouldn't damage the glass was her purse. She lobbed it up and was mortified when it landed squarely on his window ledge. The purse contained her money, credit cards and keys to her friend's flat. Anna was forced to ring the doorbell until eventually one of his sleeping friend's answered. Her man wasn't at home and she was forced to confess what she'd done. His friend looked at her like she was the maddest, baddest, bunny-boiler. This embarrassing event brought Anna to her senses when she realised this 'bad boy' type was not good for her sanity. She has avoided them since to the distinct benefit of her love life and reputation.

Sporty man: This guy loves his team sports, whether playing or watching – usually accompanied by a beer with his mates. He is instantly recognisable from his attire (either his club shirt or trakkie bottoms and trainers).

Fit bloke: This guy is bit of a narcissist and spends most of his leisure time down the gym with his mate, hogging the free weights in front of the mirrors. He's instantly identifiable by the fact that he has a preference for muscle-revealing vests and a perma tan.

Techno whiz: There's nothing this chap enjoys more then spending his waking hours glued to the TV, computer, or games console. He's instantly recognisable from the supersized TV and surround sound system.

Company man: Married to his job, this guy gets his validation from the workplace. A wife and kids are an inevitability to him at some stage, especially if he's looking to climb the corporate ladder. He can be spotted by the pristine condition of his company car and his unavailability – due to the hours he spends at work.

GET READY

Steady guy: This guy is Mr Dependable. He has his bad points like anyone else but his strength is that he's consistently there and nice and reliable.

Bad boy: A bit like chocolate, you know he's not good for you, but you can't help yourself. There are different types of bad boy: the ones who will two-time you, the ones who never return your calls and stand you up, the ones who abandon you to go out with their mates and the worst ones, who undermine your confidence and eat away at your self-esteem.

Mr Nice guy: The one guy that your mother is guaranteed to welcome with open arms. He'll never treat you badly, is always thinking of your feelings and happiness, but sometimes he's just too nice.

Flash guy: This guy has cash and he wants everyone to know it. He gets his validation from the size of his bank account and his flash car. Chances are he's already got a wife to look after his house and kids, although the ones in their 50s are often ready to 'trade up' for a younger version.

Laid-back lad: Does as little as he can possibly get away with for maximum return and accepts responsibility for very little, but can be very charming with it. These are easily identifiable by their casual attire, and are usually found indulging leisure pursuits (pub). They can lull you into a false sense of security, but avoid them unless you're looking for someone to mother.

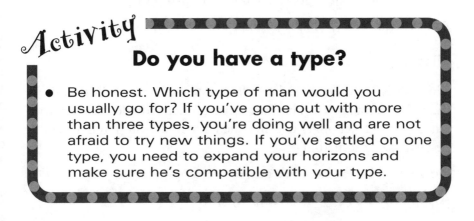

Activity
Do you have a type?

- Be honest. Which type of man would you usually go for? If you've gone out with more than three types, you're doing well and are not afraid to try new things. If you've settled on one type, you need to expand your horizons and make sure he's compatible with your type.

GET READY

What type should you pick?

Experience is a wonderful thing because it enables you to recognise a mistake when you make it again. However, in order to try and prevent you from making the same mistake again it's time for an honest appraisal of your own (tongue-in-cheek) stereotype. If you're struggling to choose, ask your friends. If you fit into more than one category, pick the one you feel is most dominant at the moment.

Cool and calm

May appear aloof at times and can be hard to please. A lady that knows her own mind, she suffers fools badly, which may give the impression that she has a short fuse. She takes care of her appearance and is usually immaculately turned out.

Go for Mr Nice guy, Flash guy, or possibly Company man.

Avoid Laid-back lad and Sporty man.

Miss Ambitious

Takes her career seriously. Her satisfaction comes from her own achievements and independence. She will put work before her relationship and will go at the glass ceiling with a sledgehammer if necessary.

Go for Company man, Flash guy, or possibly Techno whiz if you want your home network maintained in tip-top shape.

Avoid Steady guy – he hates ambitious women.

Miss Shy

This lady is as fragile as a delicate flower. She takes her validation from the people around her. The little devil on her shoulder fills her with self-doubt but her angel tells her she's a nice person. Tends always to be busy doing something.

Go for Laid-back lad, Nice guy, or Steady guy.

Avoid The Bad boy and Company man.

Yummy mummy

Has children and can still wear size 10. Drops the kids off then whizzes away from the school gates in her 4×4 to the gym. Yummy mummy can usually afford her lifestyle thanks to an ex-husband somewhere.

Go for Fit bloke, Techno whizz, or Bad boy.

Avoid Laid-back lad and Company man.

The girl next door

Sees her role in life as carer and home maker, always lends an ear and can be house proud (if she has the time). She's not a fashion victim, loves a chat, and is happy to help out with worthy causes.

Go for Steady guy, Company man, Laid-back lad or Mr Nice.

Avoid Bad boy and Flash guy.

Good-time girl

This girl is a barrel of laughs, doesn't take anything too seriously and is living for the moment. She loves a night out with the girls as much as a night in with her man. She'd be lost without her handbag, mobile, emergency pants, lippy and cash card.

Go for Sporty guy, Company man and Fit bloke.

Avoid Nice guy, Laid-back guy, Steady guy, Techno whizz and Bad boy.

Activity
Finding a perfect match

- Make a list of names of men who fancy you (past and present) and which stereotype they are. Do not only include people you've actually dated.

- Make a list of men you've got your eye on and which stereotype they are.

- This information will be useful when you start looking at your options. How easy did you find this? Can you spot your best-suited stereotype?

GET READY

Your DIY image assessment

Enough looking backwards for a while – prepare yourself for a bit of action.

The problem with image is that we don't always see ourselves as others see us.

I have to confess that I'm no style guru, my attempt at boho ended up looking more like bag lady, and with my ever-increasing bosom I'm constantly having to change my style of tops to avoid looking like a pair of walking breasts. However, I have worked with some brilliant Image Consultants.

The key to discovering your perfect style is not to become a fashion victim (unless you have unlimited time and money), but to find a look that is **authentic** to you and **appropriate** for what you're doing. Be assured that there's no such thing as the 'right' style, it's only 'your' style you have to concern yourself with.

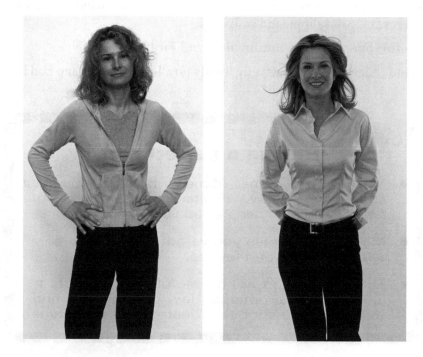

Assess your image

Before planning your new dating look, you need to ask yourself the following questions.

1. Describe an outfit or garment of yours that is authentic to your style and taste.
2. Describe an outfit or garment of yours that is appropriate for your lifestyle/occupation.
3. How do you see yourself?
4. How do you think others see you?
5. How would you like to be perceived?
6. What's your best feature?

Repeat the exercise asking your close friends to answer. (If you ask your mum you may want to take her answers with a pinch of salt – do you want to look like your mother?)

Let's take a look at Mel's answers.

1. Fluffy cardigan and tits-out top – generally a bit tarty.
2. Fluffy cardigan and suits.
3. Always slightly left of the mark, never quite hitting the spot dresswise.
4. Loud, confident, extrovert.
5. Sophisticated.
6. Big eyes and impressive cleavage.

You can see instantly that what Mel feels is her authentic style (1) is at odds with how she would like to be perceived (5). As a result she's never going to feel that she has achieved the right look, which is actually what she indicated in her answer question 3. Mel is going to need to compromise if she is to achieve a style that matches her ambitions without losing her sense of self.

GET READY

13

Your wardrobe makeover

You've had a night to mull over how you want to be portrayed and what kind of look you'll feel comfortable and confident in, let's put it into practice so you're prepared by the time we get to the 'dating options'.

> **FACT**: Men are attracted to vibrant colour and shape.

At the very least you want an outfit which makes you feel sexy, confident and attractive. There's nothing less attractive than a woman who's constantly clawing at her skirt or top because it's too tight or too short.

The capsule wardrobe

A capsule wardrobe can be made by coordinating only a few items:

- ◆ Skirt
- ◆ Pair of trousers
- ◆ Dress
- ◆ Several co-ordinated tops
- ◆ Jacket
- ◆ Cardigan
- ◆ Jumper
- ◆ Pair of flats, heels and boots
- ◆ Plus accessories.

But before you rush to the shops you need to think about:

- ◆ What suits your body shape
- ◆ Which colours suit you best
- ◆ Your budget
- ◆ Accessories to dress outfits up or down.

Use your outfit as a tool

Think of your dating outfit as a topic for conversation. You don't want it to say 'bland and boring'. You may not want it to say 'Palm reader on Blackpool pleasure beach' either!

 TOP TIP

> ◆ Use dark colours to minimise problem areas and colour to draw attention to your best areas.

GET READY

Use black to hide a problem area. Even at my skinniest I've still got saddle-bag thighs, so I tend to use a pair of black trousers to cover them and a bright coloured top with a good fitting bra to give my chest a boost.

Top the whole thing off with accessories to match the occasion. I've got a necklace with a cat face on it – it's very simple but unusual and everyone comments on it. This gives me an opportunity to thank them for the compliment or to start a conversation about cats (I'm not a lover of them) or pets in general (people can ramble on forever if they're an animal lover).

I also used to have a handbag with a whistle on it. Strangers would often ask what the whistle was for, or depending how late in the evening it was they'd be on their knees blowing it!

Give your date as many opportunities as possible to comment on your attire and be ready to accept the compliments or develop threads of conversations to follow on.

Activity

Clear out your wardrobe

- Recruit the help of a trusted but objective friend go through your wardrobe and throw out anything you haven't worn in a year or that doesn't fit you any more. Make sure she takes them straight to the charity shop so you're not tempted to slip them back into your wardrobe.

- Make a list of what you have left and what you need to compile a co-ordinating capsule wardrobe.

- Have a look at a copy of *Drab to fab* from this series, or book an appointment with a personal shopper (stores like Debenhams provide this service for free) to decide on what shapes and colours are best for you.

- Plan a budget and a timescale for assembling your capsule wardrobe (or at least a dress-to-impress outfit).

GET READY

Great hair grabs attention

A woman's hair can be her crowning glory but only if she has fab hair that looks amazing all the time. Most of us have to work for great hair. 30% of women suffer from thinning hair, which can affect confidence and self-esteem and massively restricts the choice of styles you can have without looking 'thin on top'.

For everyone else it's simply a case of finding a style that suits the way you feel and look, and is as high- or low-maintenance as you can manage.

TOP TIP

- Always keep you hair clean, and eat plenty of protein and iron-rich foods (other than disease, diet is the primary cause of poor hair).

Research

Visit the hairdressers prior to your appointment and have a leisurely flick through their selection of magazines, note your choices, then ask the hairdresser whether they will suit your face shape, whether your hair can hold the style and how much maintenance the style will take. Don't be bullied into having a style you don't want and if you don't get what you asked for, don't be afraid to complain.

Which salon?

- Unless you want to look like everyone else, avoid large franchised salons, as they teach the same cuts to all stylists.
- If your hairdresser is your bosom buddy but never gives you the new style you want, go somewhere else. If you want to go back you can always tell her you won the cut in a raffle and didn't want to waste the prize.

◆ Go for the most expensive hairdresser you can afford. You generally get what you pay for.

Colouring your hair

Being the owner of a plain brown bonce I'm a self-confessed lover of hair colour. A good colour can lift your whole appearance and self-esteem. A bad colour can put years on you and seriously affect the way that people view you.

TOP TIP

◆ Ask someone whose style you like who their hairdresser is.

◆ Never have your hair cut on the spur of the moment.

◆ Never dress down to go to the hairdressers, they'll try to match your cut to your look (which is fine if what you want to achieve is 'middle-aged dinner lady').

◆ Don't smile when you're having your fringe cut as it lifts your face and forehead. When your style is finished it may be too short.

Activity
Get your hair done

● Ask a trusted friend whether they think your look would benefit from a re-style or possibly some colour.

● Book an appointment and choose your new style.

● Go online and try some of the hairstyles out – see ukhairdressers.com for salons and styling tips.

GET READY

Quick fix – younger looking skin

The best thing you can do to look younger is look after your skin on a daily basis. When it's not maintained it looks ageing and dull. Everyone notices when it's bright and clear, and you want your skin in tip-top shape for keeping your confidence high and impressing Mr Right.

I didn't know what a skincare routine was until I was 30. I rarely even took my make-up off at night – why waste precious moments that could be better spent on sleep? I took it for granted that I'd always have my grandmother's peachy, wrinkle-free complexion. A chance encounter on a cosmetics counter gave me a daily eyecare routine that took five years off me in the space of a month. I wasn't even aware that I had puffy eyes, but by the end of the month people were commenting that they had gone, and they've never returned since. The beauty of this 60-second routine is that you don't need to use £40 eye cream, it works just as well with a £6.95 tube. Unfortunately I don't have the space here to share it with you, so pop along to your nearest make-up counter and ask them for a lesson or email me (see my address in the Introduction) and I'll send you a fact sheet. The point of this story is that with a little effort you can take years off and remain in good shape without spending a fortune or going under the knife.

If you already have a skincare routine, 10 brownie points to you, but do remember to get your skin checked out from time to time – a change in working environment or aging will affect your skin's needs. If you don't have a routine, try this one.

1 Always remove make-up before going to bed.
2 Moisturise on a daily basis to plump and hydrate.
3 Always wear sunscreen under your make-up.
4 Use a gentle exfoliator once a week to keep skin gleaming.
5 Use a mask occasionally to tone and tighten skin – the effect is only temporary but it has the added effect of keeping pores clean.

GET READY

TOP TIP

- Disguise bags and wrinkles with highlighter not concealer. Concealer will clog up wrinkles and make them look worse; highlighter will reflect the light and counter the shadows.
- Have eyebrows groomed to give the impression of lifted lids – more skin showing over the brow bone opens up the entire eye. Don't over-pluck or you'll get that 'permanently surprised' look.
- Use some light-reflecting cream under or over your make-up to get a youthful glow – most of them have the added benefit of an SPF factor. Beware not to go too overboard or you'll achieve the iridescent appearance of a fish skin.

Activity
Spruce up your skin

- Have a clearout of your make-up drawer. Throw out anything over 6 months old, it'll be full of bacteria.

- Make a point of cutting back on caffeine and alcohol or at the very least drink as much water (8 glasses a day) as you can manage.

- Book yourself a complimentary skincare makeover at a cosmetics counter. At your appointment, don't feel obliged to buy anything. However, do ask them to recommend three essential things to improve your skincare. Either get them yourself or put them on your present list.

If, like me, you struggle to find the time to get to the shops, I can recommend virginvie.co.uk – or check out any of the many online retailers.

GET READY

Ditch diets, think yourself thin

Some people believe that you can never be too rich or to thin. I say, what tosh! Where does happiness and well-being come into this ridiculous belief? Whether you're physically overweight or just 'feeling fat', letting your size bother you will simply dent your self-esteem. Follow my advice for a happier 'slimmer' you.

Physically overweight

If you are overweight then clearly for the sake of your health you must take action. I would refer you to the wisdom of my grandmother: 'Everything in moderation.' If you need impartial advice on what constitutes a balanced diet visit cancerresearchuk.org.

Most of us overeat at trigger points – to discover what your trigger points are keep a 'food and mood' diary. Note what you eat and when, and your mood at the time – you'll be surprised by the results. Once you've discovered what makes you overeat, put together a list of things to do in order to combat your triggers, e.g. phone a friend, clean the shower, sort your underwear drawer out, etc. If you have any concerns about your weight, speak to your GP.

Feeling fat

The other weight sufferers are women who are a perfectly normal weight and size – they just seem to be the only ones who can't see it. Start to see yourself as everyone else sees you – you're a great-looking individual. Take a look around and you'll see there are plenty of people whose figures you wouldn't want to have. If seeing lots of images of thin women in the press depresses you then don't look at them – and remember that most of them have had plastic surgery, have an entourage of people to maintain their image or have simply been airbrushed. Surround yourself with pictures of yourself that you like. Try only looking in mirrors from the chest up and you can banish your body-shape issues from your mind in an instant.

GET READY

If there's someone eating away at your self-confidence by telling you you're fat, then simply avoid them or find their Achilles heel and give them a taste of their own medicine.

As long as your weight isn't a threat to your health, don't think of it as an inhibitor to finding love, just get on with it using the strategies above.

⊙ TOP TIP

♦ Make sure you have a large glass of water when you're hungry between meals. Sometimes it's actually thirst which makes you think you're hungry.

Activity
Focus on your good points

● Make a list of your best features and stick it on the mirror.

● Read your list every day and compliment yourself on your good features.

● Banish negative thoughts about your body – if you start to put yourself down go back to your list.

● Avoid people who dent your self-esteem.

● Make a commitment to do this every day and you'll be giving off a sex-goddess vibe by the time you meet Mr Right.

GET READY

Are you keeping up? Do you need some help? If you've not already subscribed, why not try the daily text messaging service for extra encouragement and support. Just text 'Settled 11' to 80881 now.

Each set of messages costs £1.50. Please see page x for full terms and conditions.

Pit stop 1 – take stock

'A pessimist sees the difficulty in every opportunity; an optimist sees the opportunity in every difficulty.' Winston Churchill

A picture paints a thousand words, so what we're going to do today is transfer all the work you've done in Days 1 to 10 into a diagram so you can see which areas need more work. You can also refer back to it later on to see what's improved.

Determination

On Day 1 we looked at all the excuses you could be giving for not finding a new man. Since then you've been telling yourself, 'There's a man out there for me and I'm going to find him'. On Day 3 we looked at your dating habits and how to beat them. On a scale of 1 to 10, with 1 being the lowest and 10 being the highest, shade in your level of determination to succeed.

Body image

On Day 10 we looked at how you perceive your own body size. In your own mind are you 'fat and fabulous' or 'never thin enough'? Keep on re-affirming all your great attributes and shade in on the scale how happy you are with your body image.

Wardrobe

On Days 6 and 7 we looked at how your choice of clothes could work for or against you. You've uncluttered your wardrobe and left a lovely clear canvas for you to work with, aiming for a look that is authentic to your personal style and appropriate for your lifestyle. Shade in where you think you are in terms of getting it right, 1 being 'miles off' and 10 being 'spot on'.

GET READY

Hair and make-up

On Days 8 and 9 we looked at your crowning glory and your skin care. Have these steps improved the way you feel about your hair and make-up now? Shade in your response on the chart.

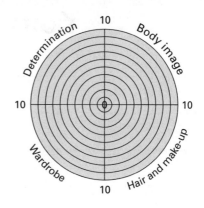

⊙✎ TOP TIP

◆ To get the most accurate picture, do this when you have 5 minutes of uninterrupted time and when you're feeling at your most perky.

Activity
Today's activity

● Look at which areas are the lowest on your chart – this is where you need to be focusing more of your efforts. Go back to the relevant Days and make sure you're doing the activities as instructed. You'll get there soon enough.

● Give yourself a big pat on the back for areas where you're doing well. Ideally you want all areas to be above a 7, but it's all relative to you. Everyone has their own internal yard stick – the point is that you have to feel you've scored the best you can to your satisfaction (regardless of what anyone else may score).

GET READY

Your notes

....
....
....
....
....
....
....
....
....
....
....
....
....
....
....
....

CHAPTER 2

GET SET

Consider your dating options

'The only thing that stands between a man and what he wants from life is often merely the will to try it and the faith to believe that it is possible.' David Viscott, psychiatrist

What we're going to look at today are the factors that will influence what types of avenues you might want to go down when looking for Mr Right. Looking for a date is a bit like looking for a new job – there are many options open to you, you just have to find which ones are most convenient for you and offer the best likelihood of success.

I'm afraid this involves a bit of 'suck it and see' to start with. You wouldn't look for a new job and use only one method, e.g. the local paper. If you wanted to increase the chances of getting your top job, you'd register with agencies, go online and register with the job boards, get the trade/professional magazine with industry-specific jobs, ask around, etc. The same is true of finding a date – you've got to put it about to get about.

There are three determining factors.

Budget

Filthy lucre has to come into it somewhere – there aren't many things you get for free that are worth anything. How much cash can you afford to splash?

Time

You'll probably have limited time due to work, home commitments, hobbies, etc. You'll need time to prepare your personal information then submit it. Dating events are time-consuming as are dates themselves. Advance consideration needs to be given to the time management of your dating activities.

Location

Whether you live in the smoke or the sticks will also influence the effectiveness of your dating options.

⊙— TOP TIP

- If you're new to the area, work out your dating location. Find out where the nearest large towns are and draw a ring around them on a map to make sure your radius isn't too small.

Activity
What are your limits?

- Set yourself a budget for the next three months (until you've finished this guide) for how much you can afford to spend on dating activities.

  £ _____ per month

- Decide how much free time you have available to spend on dating activities (including the dates themselves).

  _____ hours per week

- Look at your location and set yourself a radius within which you are prepared to date.

  _____ miles

Composing your 'Yellow pages' ad

TOP TIP

◆ Keep it positive.

Today we're going to summarise you in a nutshell. You're going to have to be able to 'sell' yourself quickly and succinctly, getting all the best bits across and making yourself a highly desirable proposition for the right man.

Start by reading the 'would like to meet' section of a paper or on the internet – see what sort of things men are looking for. There is a subtle difference between what men want and what women want. Most men will describe the physical attributes of the sort of woman they want (tall, slim, blonde, etc), whereas women look for the more touchy feely aspects of a man (good sense of humour, non-smoker, kind to small furry animals, etc). However, what men think they want and what they actually go for can often be completely different.

CASE STUDY

I had one client who was male, early thirties, confident, funny, average looks, slim and very fit. He was looking for a 25–30 tall, slim (size 10) blonde, with intellect, dazzling personality and financial independence. He's actually very happily settled down with a 34-year-old 5' 6" brunette, size 14–16, who's level-headed and often grumpy at the end of her busy day as a doctor.

Someone once told me that 'in any conversation someone is buying and someone is selling' – this has never been truer of the dating game. It's growing into a massive multi-million pound industry, and those who learn how to sell themselves well will have the biggest choice of dates and be the quickest to success.

FACT: Research shows that the relationships that are most likely to last longest are where a couple are matched lookswise.

GET SET

Activity ●●●●●●●●●●●●●●●●●●
Advertise yourself

- Remembering to keep it positive, fill in a description of yourself under each of the following headings:
  - Physical characteristics
  - Personality
  - Personal circumstances
  - Hobbies and interests.

- If there are any aspects of you that you feel aren't very flattering or attractive to the opposite sex, simply omit them. Men generally go for attributes, so use lots of descriptive adjectives: for 'plump' substitute 'curvaceous' or 'rubenesque', for 'skinny' use 'slender' or 'svelte', for 'small', 'petite', for 'tall', 'statuesque', etc. 'Statuesque lady with wavy brunette locks and big brown eyes' sounds more attractive than 'tall, dark, brown-eyed female'. A lot of men discriminate against lone-parent families, so if you don't have to mention you have children, then don't – unless you're specifically looking for a father figure for your children rather than a date for yourself.

- Now turn your notes into a paragraph the size of a 'Yellow pages' advert (below). This will be your baseline 'sales pitch' for use in all the following sections.

> **My 'Yellow pages' ad**
> _____
> _____
> _____
> _____
> _____

GET SET

29

The perfect 'Would like to meet' ad

Today you're going to lay out who exactly you would like to meet. You'll need this information for most activities over the coming days, so it's worth preparing it in advance.

TOP TIP

- The more flexible you are the more likely you are to attract a range of dates to choose from.

CASE STUDY

I went to a speed dating event once and was amazed at half-time when a rather grumpy, chubby, trainee teacher was bitching about the quality of the men (most of whom were perfectly acceptable to my mind). She was looking for a tall, handsome high-earner, with a great sense of humour, and an immediate desire to get married and father children (so she would never again have to set foot inside a classroom – except as a parent). I had to titter to myself that I'd never seen any man fitting her description advertising for 'plain, portly, whiners' and therefore her quest was somewhat doomed from the outset.

If you don't want to suffer the same disappointment, follow the advice below.

TOP TIP

- Have a look on the internet and in the 'would like to meet' section in your paper. Pick out the ads which you feel are most eye-catching and portray the sort of man whom you would like to meet.

Your description should be split into the following topics/preferences:

- Physical characteristics, e.g. height, weight, hair (or not), build, etc.
- Personality type, e.g. serious, easygoing, intense, good sense of humour, patient, etc.

GET SET

- Personal circumstances, e.g. single, divorced, with/no kids, own home, etc.
- Hobbies and interests, e.g. type of music, sports, theatre, food, etc.
- Type of relationship, e.g. friends at first, no strings, marriage partner, etc.
- Location, e.g. within 5 miles of (town), within (region), etc.

Start by make some bullet points, then construct a paragraph. Here's an example of a very straight-talking 'would like to meet'. Yours may not be as direct as this, but try to make it as distinctive and eye-catching as possible and incorporate as much of 'you' into your ad as possible.

> 'Would like to meet: tall, professional, athletically-built man, preferably orphaned or with parents who have emigrated. Must like children, either with none of his own or grown-up offspring. Age and location unimportant. Sense of humour essential, patience of a saint beneficial, passion for everything critical.'

'Would like to meet' turn-offs

There are certain unscrupulous men that will prey on vulnerable-sounding women. Using negative language will attract them and put off the men you would like to attract. Never use the following terms:

- Lonely
- Broken-hearted
- Nervous
- Easily hurt
- Shy.

Activity Write your ad

- Get a clean sheet of paper and compose your 'would like to meet' advert following the advice above and bearing in mind the types of men you should be avoiding. Aim for as much information as possible at first, then refine it to whichever application you're using it for.

GET SET

How to sound just right

We've covered how to say the right things on paper, now we need to make your voice sound as attractive as you are. At some stage you'll have to talk to an answer machine or leave a voice message for potential suitors. I don't know many people who sound alluring on such low-quality recordings without a bit of help.

Do you get people that leave you messages sounding like they need a good dose of Prozac? Does the sound of their flat nasaly whine make you want to rush to the receiver to call them back? No. And that's the effect you're going to have if you don't follow this really simple activity.

Where most people become unintelligible is when they don't pronounce their consonants. Last year I wrote and narrated an Audio CD of practical flirting advice and steps called Flirt Guru. Much to my surprise, despite the

> **FACT:** If you sound dull and flat on a recorded message, you are far less likely to be called back.

CD being less than an hour it actually took several days to record to get my voice sounding consistent and the narration clear. The problem was that I normally talk quickly and I didn't notice that I dropped my consonants on the end of words – in order for people to be able to follow the CD I had to speak more slowly, which made my bad speech habit much worse. An excellent voice coach got me to read my script slowly with a wine cork between my teeth, forming each word properly. Lo and behold, when I removed the cork I could say the words perfectly!

The thought that this could be 'the one' will get your pulse racing when replying to any messages, so make sure you take a moment to slow down. Answer machines also have a nasty habit of making us sound very serious and terminally depressed.

GET SET

To avoid this, warm your voice up in advance. Sing a nursery rhyme in a pitch that is higher than you would normally sing. Give it a couple of goes through until your voice is used to the higher range. When you say your message make your voice almost 'sing songy' and say it much slower than you would normally – you may feel silly doing it but when you play it back, it will sound surprisingly 'normal' and will be very pleasing on the ear.

TOP TIP

- Slow your voice down.
- Use a 'sing song' tone.
- Form your consonants.

Activity

Leave a perfect message

Practise leaving a message on your answer machine at home or on your mobile.

- First write a script.

- Go through the warm-up exercises above.

- Keep re-recording and playing back your message until you get one that makes you sound attractive, happy and the sort of person you want to call back immediately.

GET SET

Your notes

....

....

....

....

....

....

....

....

....

....

....

....

....

....

CHAPTER 3

GO! QUICK-START DATING OPTIONS

Speed dating

The great thing about speed dating is it's a bit like job interviews – the more times you do it, the better you get.

What is it?

Speed dating is an event where a number of men and women are introduced to each other on a series (between 10 and 30) of mini dates, usually lasting 3–5 minutes (depending on the numbers involved).

How does it work?

Everyone is given a number and a tick sheet, and seated with a member of the opposite sex. When the bell goes one party moves round and you meet your next date. You secretly mark on your card whether you would like to see that person again, then at the end of the event the cards are collected and the organiser works out your matches. Some organisers give out the results straight away, others do it after the event, usually by e-mail or posted on a website. None of your details are given to anyone you don't want to see again.

Do I have to be a member?

Generally speaking, no – you can pick and choose events according to your location and availability.

How much does it cost?

Between £10 and £20 per event.

Location effect?

You will get more choice if you are prepared to travel to a city or large town.

Where can I find speed dating events?

There are a few large web–based companies which run events all over the country. Some bars run their own events and there are often charity events advertised in local papers.

Common fears

◆ **What if nobody picks me?** Ladies are far choosier than men. Men tick far more 'Yes's than 'No's, so although you may not have chosen many, it's unlikely that nobody will have chosen you.

◎⟵ TOP TIP

- ◆ Create your own e-mail account. Try www.yahoo.co.uk for a step-by-step guide.
- ◆ If you want to find out how generally attractive you are, tick 'Yes' to everyone and you'll see who ticked your card.
- ◆ Lots of people go on their own, but if you can't face it take a friend. They can always wait in the bar.
- ◆ Try these national speed dating companies:
  – www.speeddater.co.uk
  – www.chemistry.co.uk

✐ctivity
Your first speed dates

- ● Find your nearest event and arrange to go.

- ● Decide on your outfit in advance (most people go from work, so office-wear is fine, but remember you want to dress to impress).

- ● Start preparing topics for conversation and practise your questions on the people around you. You may get some more ideas for expanding the conversation.

GO! QUICK-START DATING OPTIONS

Singles clubs/nights

Singles clubs are today's focus. Long gone are the image of grab-a-granny nights down the local hotel, crammed wall-to-wall with men working away from home and ladies of a certain age. The rapid growth of the dating industry and internet advertising has given this well-trodden activity a whole new lease of life.

> **FACT:** The purpose of singles nights is to get single people together, not terrify the life out of participants.

What is it?

An organised event aimed at single people. It can be anything from a midnight walk across a beach, to a dinner, or even a large event in a club. Chemistry has emerged over the last couple of years as **the** event organiser in the UK for large events – there are lots of different activities at each, to appeal to all types of singletons.

How does it work?

You register and pay for the event in advance.

Do I have to be a member?

You don't have to be a member to go along to these events but you will need to register and pay in advance. However, local dating agencies often hold dinners and supper evenings are usually reserved for members.

How much does it cost?

A singles night at an event like Chemistry costs about £20. However you can expect to pay more for dinners.

Location effect?

If you live in the sticks local events are likely to be smaller and tend to vary according to the organiser – they may stick to their tried and tested 'granny nights'. If you can make it into a city centre the large events attract big crowds, many of whom come from outside the area for the increased choice of participants.

Where can I find it?

Traditional singles nights are advertised in the local papers, local dating agencies will advertise their own to their members and national events like chemistry are promoted by other agencies and also on their own website (www3.chemistry.co.uk).

Common fears

◆ **I'm worried about attending an event on my own.** This is a fear shared by the vast majority of people attending these events. The organisers are well used to coping with new participants and putting them at their ease.

TOP TIP

- ◆ To avoid 'granny nights', contact the event organiser prior to booking and ask about the male/female split and the average age of participants.

Activity

Sample a singles night

- ● Find your nearest singles events and contact the organisers to establish which ones are going to be most appropriate for you.

- ● If it's within your budget, book yourself a place to go.

GO! QUICK-START DATING OPTIONS

39

Singles holidays

An old idea with a fashionable new acceptability, singles holidays no longer say 'on the shelf' about you, and you can do anything from white water rafting to yoga retreats.

What is it?

Singles breaks can be anything from a weekend away in the UK to a full-blown holiday abroad. Generally they are for single people but some organisations also include single people not looking for love.

How does it work?

An organiser gathers a party of like-minded people together for the event of their choice.

Do I have to be a member?

Some dating organisations offer this service and would expect you to be a member to participate. However, there are many organisations that offer holidays for single people where membership is not required.

How much does it cost?

The cost really depends on the type of activity you undertake. A week's skiing is going to be more expensive than a week in the sun.

Location effect?

If you're looking to go overseas your location is irrelevant. If you are looking for local weekend walking events, for example, then there is going to be more choice the larger your town of residence.

Where can I find it?

Singles holidays are advertised through dating agencies to their members and also on the internet. Your local travel agent will also be able to recommend a service to you.

TOP TIP

- Check out these websites for ideas on break/holiday options.
  - www.twistedmartini.co.uk
  - www.solosholidays.co.uk/
  - www.solitairhols.co.uk
  - www.spiceuk.com

Common fears

What if I don't fancy any of the other people on the trip? This is always going to be a risk, but as you are under no pressure to 'pull' you can just enjoy the break in the company of the group. Organisers appreciate that you need your own space and this is taken into consideration when planning the trip.

Activity
What holidays tempt you?

- Research the singles holidays organisers who are most appropriate to your holiday preferences.

- See if any of them do late booking offers.

- If you've got the budget and time galore, book it now, otherwise keep the information safe for later. (You may have found Mr Right by the time the holiday comes round.)

GO! QUICK-START DATING OPTIONS

Introduction agencies

Despite all the technology-based applications available, the old-fashioned introduction agency exists for those people whose time is precious and who wish to outsource the process of looking for a date. Despite the initially high price tag it often turns out to be the most cost-effective method.

What is it?

Trained consultants look for a partner on your behalf.

How does it work?

You have an interview with a consultant, then from the information you've given them and their experience of matching people, they select a number of people for your consideration. You will be provided with a profile of each and be secure in the knowledge that they have been interviewed and identity-checked.

Do I have to be a member?

Yes.

How much does it cost?

This varies from agency to agency. Anything from a few hundred to a few thousand pounds.

Location effect?

Due to the high cost of this type of selection process, for the best choice of candidates, either choose a long-established reputable local agency or a high-profile national agency that does a lot of advertising or has a portfolio of other dating offerings, e.g. Avenues dating.

Where can I find it?

On the internet and in the 'Yellow pages' and most national papers, e.g. *The Sunday Times* 'Encounters' section, and regional papers.

Common fears

What if I spend all this money and they don't find a match?
A reputable agency will let you know in advance if they feel they don't have anyone meeting your specification.

TOP TIP

♦ Ask if they have any offers on – agencies will sometimes offer you a special deal. The end of the month/quarter is a good time to try this.

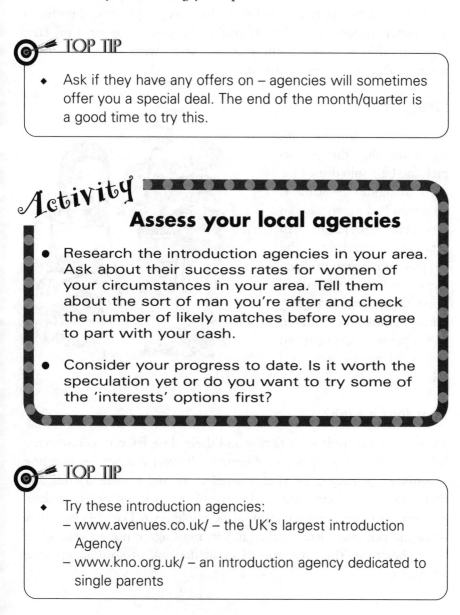

Activity

Assess your local agencies

● Research the introduction agencies in your area. Ask about their success rates for women of your circumstances in your area. Tell them about the sort of man you're after and check the number of likely matches before you agree to part with your cash.

● Consider your progress to date. Is it worth the speculation yet or do you want to try some of the 'interests' options first?

TOP TIP

♦ Try these introduction agencies:
  – www.avenues.co.uk/ – the UK's largest introduction Agency
  – www.kno.org.uk/ – an introduction agency dedicated to single parents

GO! QUICK-START DATING OPTIONS

Friend and family referral

We're leaving no stone unturned in our review of your options, and today we're going to look at what some may consider the unthinkable – your family choosing a date for you. I could have put it nearer the start of the dating options but I thought most people would prefer to give other options a go first. If you're short of funds, or a bit lazy, however, this is an excellent place to start, with no phone calls, internet, fees, or events to attend.

What is it?

In some cultures it's traditional that the parents pick the best-suited man for their daughter – this is commonly known as an arranged marriage. In arranged marriages the couples often feel that the family are best placed to know them better than they know themselves, and to pick a partner most matched to their personality and values.

How does it work?

Your parents consult with family and their close friends to research a list of suitable dates for you. Alternatively, you can set up a dating committee consisting of your trusted male and female friends and they will search their combined networks to pick a shortlist of dates for you. You put together a list of desirables (see Day 14) and they score the potential dates against it. You must agree not to veto all of their choices or they will soon balk at the task of coming up with another list.

Do I have to be a member?

No.

How much does it cost?

Nothing.

Location effect?

If you've relocated away from home, your parents may have a more limited choice of men to choose from within a commutable distance of yourself.

Where can I find it?

Just ask.

Common fears

I feel silly asking my parents or friends to do this for me. Nonsense, they will feel honoured that you hold them in high enough regard to be trusted with such a task.

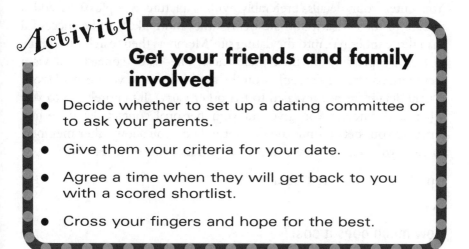

Activity

Get your friends and family involved

- Decide whether to set up a dating committee or to ask your parents.

- Give them your criteria for your date.

- Agree a time when they will get back to you with a scored shortlist.

- Cross your fingers and hope for the best.

GO! QUICK-START DATING OPTIONS

Are you keeping up? Do you need some help? If you've not already subscribed, why not try the daily text messaging service for extra encouragement and support. Just text 'Settled 21' to 80881 now.

Each set of messages costs £1.50. Please see page x for full terms and conditions.

Internet dating

If you tried internet dating a couple of years ago and weren't impressed, it's come a long way since then, so don't be put of giving it another go.

◆   If your technical skills leave something to be desired, call your local library and ask if they do any free sessions on how to use the internet.

What is it?

All your details are stored on an internet site, and limited access to them (i.e. not your contact details) is given to people looking for someone matching your description.

How does it work?

You enter your details, preferably with a picture (people who add a picture to their description are many times more likely to be successful than those tht don't), into the dating site. Members then search on a range of terms depending on their preferences. The 'dates' contact you via a secure messaging service, either on the dating site or to your e-mail (your e-mail details are not revealed to the other party). It's entirely up to you when and whether you give out your personal contact details. When entering your details onto the site not only do you allow other members to view you, but your are also able to conduct you own searches.

Do I have to be a member?

Yes.

How much does it cost?

Some sites are free, but you generally only get what you pay for. The rest range from a monthly fee to a quarterly subscription.

Location effect?

Most people have some kind of internet access, if not from home, then the office or an internet café. If you live in a remote area be prepared to extend your radius to give you the best possible selection of men.

Where can I find it?

Put 'dating' into the internet and you'll be inundated with options.

Common fears

How do I know that they are who they say they are? You don't know, so you must follow the safety tips on the site (see also Day 65).

CASE STUDY

Karen was extremely time-limited and decided that internet dating best suited her busy lifestyle. She was impressed with the choice of candidates and built up an e-mail rapport with one guy in particular. She eventually swapped mobile phone numbers and when they spoke the bond strengthened. When they eventually met she was bitterly disappointed – his photo about 15 years out of date. But she persisted and met the man of her dreams – 12 months on they're living happily together.

Activity

Try dating online

- Ask your friends if they can recommend any good dating sites for the area. Alternatively, try out three or four of the bigger sites to see which search facilities are better and who has the best men in your area.

- If they have a trial membership, go for it. If not, go for a month's membership. If you decide in the first week you don't like it, under consumer rights (as you've bought it over the internet) you can cancel and ask for your money back.

GO! QUICK-START DATING OPTIONS

Video phone dating

This is a very new and growing phenomenon. In order to explain today's task, I've spoken to the companies behind the launch of video phone dating, Three and Dateline.

What is it?

Video dating straight to your phone

How does it work?

You will be asked to leave your age and location using the interactive maps. You can then record a short video profile. You will receive a text message activating your membership. You will receive a free text when there is a Match for you. A search is made on your behalf every day. Call back to watch your Matches – you can reply to them if you like them. You will receive a free text message informing you of any responses to your profile. Your account is protected with a pin number.

Do I have to be a member?

It's currently a pay per use service only available through Dateline.

How much does it cost?

25p per minute. Call 89799 on any 3G-enabled phone

Location effect

The take-up of the video phone technology and coverage will have an impact on the numbers available to start with.

Where can I find it?

www.dateline.co.uk/mobile for a demo or call 89799 to subscribe.

Common fear

My contact details will be made available to the people accessing my video message. The messaging is all done through a secure system and none of your personal details are divulged. You choose when you wish to give them out.

Activity

Find out more

- Check out the press and the internet for progress on this service and new providers.

- Subscribe to the service if you wish to see more than a static photo and a text description.

Perfect your performance by recording your video message straight to your phone and playing it back before submitting it.

GO! QUICK-START DATING OPTIONS

Personal ads columns

What is it?

You can either place adverts or respond to adverts in the newspaper.

How does it work?

Most publications have moved to telephone-based systems, although *The Times* does still offer a written PO Box response service for a small charge. You place your ad for free, then collect your messages from a premium-rate number once the publication is out.

Do I have to be a member?

No.

How much does it cost?

It's generally free to place, but to pick up your messages or respond to other adverts you will have to dial a premium-rate number.

Location effect?

All locations are covered by a local/regional paper that has local people advertising.

Where can I find it?

In local free sheets, regional papers, and most national newspapers, e.g. *The Sunday Times* has a large section called 'Encounters'.

Common fears

I'll be tracked down by an axe murderer. Follow the safety guidelines given in the newspaper (and see Day 65) and you will be fine.

⦿✦ TOP TIP

> ◆ Keep old copies of the paper to check who has been advertising previously. Don't apply to old adverts as they probably aren't picking up their messages and you'll just blow your budget.

Don't forget to practise sounding delicious as per Day 15, and prepare your response to ads – mirror what your prospective date is looking for.

Get advertising

● Find out which publications' advertisers best match the type of person you're looking for.

● Check how much it costs per minute to retrieve or respond to adverts and work out how much you want to spend per week of your budget.

● Place your ad (use your 'would like to meet' ad from Day 14) and respond to any that look promising (use your 'Yellow pages' ad from Day 13).

GO! QUICK-START DATING OPTIONS

Strike a pose – getting a perfect picture

Today's section is about getting a perfect picture of yourself. If you haven't realised it before now, I have to tell you that the dreaded photo is a necessary evil. Men are physiologically attracted – it doesn't matter how sparkling your personality is in print or on the phone, they want to make sure you're not totally hideous before they'll willingly agree to a date.

Despite all the advice to the contrary, most women won't part with a photo straight away. However, it's easier than ever to pave the way with a digital photograph. If you don't have a digital camera, you can use a film one and ask for the prints on disk when you get it processed.

CASE STUDY

When renewing my passport recently I wanted the picture to be as youthful as possible. I was carrying a few extra pounds (as indeed I do on a daily basis) but decided I wanted one of those pointy little chins that ladies in their twenties have (the effect could be achieved by pulling the skin behind my ears, but this was not an acceptable passport pose). To cut a long story short, I ended up taping my chin to my ears and then round the back of my neck. Had it not been unusually hot I would probably have brazened out the trip to the photobooth sporting a scarf to cover the tape.

Common sense won the day and I abandoned the tape idea, but used up the maximum amount of shots on the machine perfecting the 'turtle just emerging from its shell' look. As it turned out, the process of putting my photo onto my passport stretched my face widthways, so I now have a face the shape of one of those square satellite dishes!

There are loads of free or very cheap image altering packages around. Most printers come with free software, and if you have a look through the selection of computer mags at the newsagents you'll find that there's always one with photosoftware on it. Alternatively, nip to your local PC World and get a cheap, low-spec version. Or you could ask to borrow a friend's (preferably one who knows how to use it).

TOP TIP

◆ Save your photo as a jpeg or a gif file. If you want to e-mail it to a perspective date, make sure you save it as a low resolution photo, otherwise it will clog up their e-mail.

Activity

Painless plastic surgery

● Take your photo and make any of the following improvments that are necessary digitally.

– If you look a bit chubby, stretch the picture longways – it'll give you instant height and melt the pounds away.
– If you have any blemishes or bags, zoom in on these areas and use the smudge feature to erase them or blend them to insignificance.
– For hips like saddlebags, zoom in then chop them off by covering over the excess with a sample of colour from the area immediately next to the part you are shading.
– Fix any red eye with the red eye corrector.
– Whiten teeth by zooming in and selecting the colour from the brightest part of teeth, then colouring and smudging the rest of them for a bit of free virtual cosmetic dentistry.

● Get it uploaded onto any of the sites you've registered with and send it to anyone you've been conversing with on e-mail. You'll be surprised at the results.

● Get a nice frame and put a copy of your photo in pride of place in your home.

GO! QUICK-START DATING OPTIONS

Pit stop 2 – summing up your options

This isn't the end of your dating options, but that's enough to get you started. Today you're going to sum up your progress so far – you'll review things again on Day 55.

Activity	Happened / due to happen	Degree of success	Future consider-ations	Day 55
'Would like to meet' ad				
'Yellow pages' ad				
Voice message				
Photo				
Speed dating				
Singles clubs				
Singles holidays				
Introduction agencies				
Friends and family				
Internet dating				
Phone dating				
Personal ads				

How much progress you've made depends on your budget, location and spare time. Don't worry if you've not cracked all of them yet, it's been a lot of work in a short period of time and you should congratulate yourself on the effort you've made to date.

Remember, activities like internet dating are probably going to run over the next three months, speed dating gets better and easier the more you do it, etc. Don't think that once you've attempted it that's it – there's quite a lifespan in a number of these activities.

Activity

How are you doing?

- Critically review your progress to date and make notes on future progress in the table opposite.

- How are you feeling about your progress. Great? OK? Could work harder? Give yourself a pat on the back for the progress you've made so far.

- Make a 'treasure map'. Use a large piece of paper or a bulletin board. Half of the board represents your wishes for yourself (cover it with words and pictures cut from magazines and newspapers, anything that represents your desire for yourself) and the other half is for the lifestyle you want (the type of house, kids, holidays, job, boyfriend, travel, charity work, whatever). This will help you visualise your dreams and take them one step closer to becoming a reality.

GO! QUICK-START DATING OPTIONS

Your notes

CHAPTER 4

TAKE AN IN-DEPTH LOOK

Taking a more in-depth approach

Today we're going to start looking at your approach in a little more depth. You've had an accelerated start in this programme – there's nothing more demotivating than spending ages before you get to the action. If you've been fortunate, you'll have had a couple of lucky opportunities already. In which case please keep on pursuing them, but don't forget to keep reading to make sure your dating etiquette doesn't let you down, and to consider the trigger points for deciding when he moves on from being just a date to a serious prospect.

Over the next few days we're going to look at the tried and tested elements of the Flirt Guru method. This is a strategy that was devised from working with hundreds of single professional people. They were looking for a different approach from the woolly tree-hugging stuff. 'If you love yourself everyone else will love you' is fine – if you've got all the time in the world. Besides, most people who advocate this approach wear tie dye, wash their hair only once a week (whether it needs it or not) and date bearded men sporting Jesus sandals. Mine is a forward-looking approach which focuses on getting it right in the future.

TOP TIP

> ◆ Don't forget to keep repeating the post-its on your mirror every day or whenever you pass them.

The Flirt Guru method basically consists of three phases.

Phase 1 Getting yourself in the right mind-set and getting yourself noticed for the right reasons. Days 27–30.

Phase 2 How to talk to absolutely anybody with confidence and without fear. Days 47–51.

Phase 3 Body language secrets and signs, how to read and react to them. Days 45–46 and 52–54.

Once you've got to grips with all this you'll be able to tackle just about anything with a bit of practice.

TAKE AN IN-DEPTH LOOK

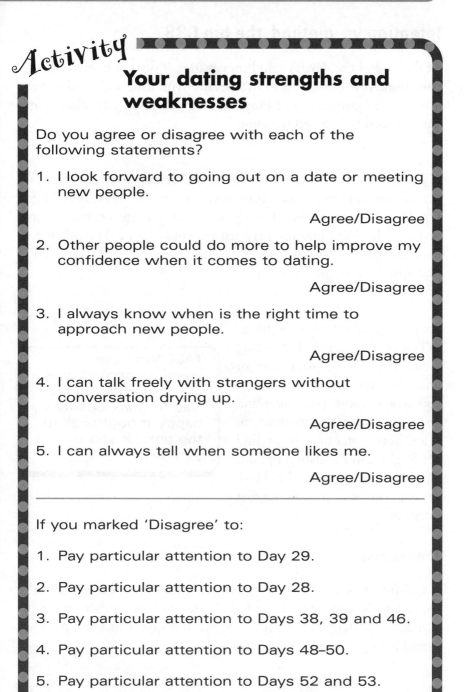

Activity

Your dating strengths and weaknesses

Do you agree or disagree with each of the following statements?

1. I look forward to going out on a date or meeting new people.

Agree/Disagree

2. Other people could do more to help improve my confidence when it comes to dating.

Agree/Disagree

3. I always know when is the right time to approach new people.

Agree/Disagree

4. I can talk freely with strangers without conversation drying up.

Agree/Disagree

5. I can always tell when someone likes me.

Agree/Disagree

If you marked 'Disagree' to:

1. Pay particular attention to Day 29.

2. Pay particular attention to Day 28.

3. Pay particular attention to Days 38, 39 and 46.

4. Pay particular attention to Days 48–50.

5. Pay particular attention to Days 52 and 53.

TAKE AN IN-DEPTH LOOK

Intention vs. method, the big CSS

At the end of the day it's mind over matter, it doesn't matter whether you think you can or you can't because you'll be right either way! Today we're going to start programming you to feel confident, sexy and successful (CSS) **all** the time.

If you don't feel CSS at the moment, it's because you've not made it part of your intention. The choice is yours – do you want to feel CSS? Or do you want to feel average, less than average or, even worse, invisible? It's like choosing between chocolate and cold mash, there's no competition. Now that it's your intention to be CSS you need to find a method of getting there.

Suppose your intention is to go to France – the method of getting there is by boat, plane, car or train. Whatever you do in life, you won't realise your intention without having the methods in place. Your intention is to find Mr Right, and the dating options plus the other tips in this book are your methods of realising that intention.

> **FACT:** We have absolute control over our thoughts. You're free to think positive, happy thoughts all of the time, if you let yourself.

The method

◆ Confident people have great posture – they always stand tall, with head high, back straight and chest out. Act as though you're the most important person in the room. It'll give you great presence and help you ooze confidence.

TAKE AN IN-DEPTH LOOK

◆ You don't have to go licking the rim of your glass like a rabid Alsatian to catch the attention of the men around you. It's not about wearing skin-tight, crotch-skimming clothes either. Sexy people are comfortable in their own skin, they laugh and smile freely and make lots of eye contact.

◆ You've heard the expressions 'dress for success' and 'dress for the job you want, not the one you have' – the same goes for looking successful. If you go round dressed as a bag lady, people are likely to treat you as one. However, I'm not suggesting you go for the power suit unless it's appropriate for what you do. Don't save dressing well for special occasions – you're special every day so make the effort on a daily basis. Not only will you feel better about your appearance, but you may impress someone special that you didn't expect to meet.

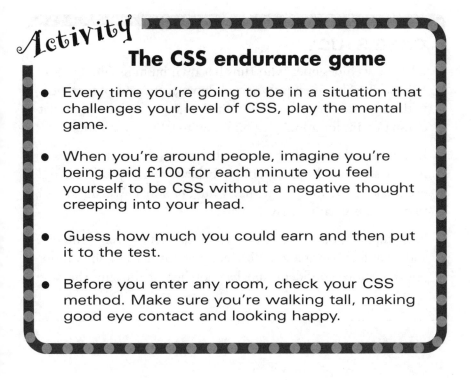

Activity

The CSS endurance game

● Every time you're going to be in a situation that challenges your level of CSS, play the mental game.

● When you're around people, imagine you're being paid £100 for each minute you feel yourself to be CSS without a negative thought creeping into your head.

● Guess how much you could earn and then put it to the test.

● Before you enter any room, check your CSS method. Make sure you're walking tall, making good eye contact and looking happy.

TAKE AN IN-DEPTH LOOK

Growing your self-esteem

'Losers visualise the penalties of failure. Winners visualise the rewards of success.' Dr Rob Gilbert

Today we're going to get a bit self-helpy, and have a look at self-esteem. People with low self-esteem/confidence are biased against themselves. Therefore they look for signs that confirm their beliefs and ignore signs that deny it.

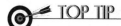 **TOP TIP**

◆ If you tell yourself that you're never going to find the right man, it's very likely to become true.

CASE STUDY

Julie is a web designer who runs her own business. She has low self-esteem. She often puts herself down at the end of sentences with little asides such as '… but that's only my opinion and that doesn't count for a lot,' '… you know me, I'm always stupid.'

It may be said in a joking manner, but your subconscious doesn't have a sense of humour and it believes what you're saying, eventually persuading you that your opinion is worthless and that you are what you say you are.

Julie stopped putting herself down at the end of every sentence and now feels completely differently about herself. She's more positive, more confident and has got herself the guy she was after.

TAKE AN IN-DEPTH LOOK

Activity

Your self-esteem

- Answer the following questions with A, B, C, and D, where

  A = Strongly agree   C = Disagree
  B = Agree   D = Strongly disagree

  1. Generally speaking I'm happy with myself. ____
  2. Sometimes I think I'm absolutely worthless. ____
  3. I'm as capable as most people. ____
  4. I feel I'm a bit of a failure. ____
  5. I feel positive about myself. ____
  6. I'd like to have more respect for myself. ____

- Calculate your score using the grid below.

Scoring

1. a) 2   b) 1   c) –1   d) –2
2. a) –2   b) –1   c) 1   d) 2
3. a) 2   b) 1   c) –1   d) –2
4. a) –2   b) –1   c) 1   d) 2
5. a) 2   b) 1   c) –1   d) –2
6. a) –2   b) –1   c) 1   d) 2

8–12: You're fine!
6–8: You're OK, but you need to keep an eye on which areas you're negative about and keep them in check.
5 or less: Ask a friend in which areas they think you are being unfairly hard on yourself – are you putting yourself down? Identifing the problem is half the battle. Work on being more positive in these areas.

TAKE AN IN-DEPTH LOOK

Every day is an opportunity

'Success is not the result of spontaneous combustion. You must set yourself on fire.' Reggie Leach, Canadian hockey player, 1950

Today we're going to look at the benefits of the old Scout motto 'Be prepared'. Preparation makes life so much easier. It's taken me approximately 30 years finally to agree with this statement. I've never prepared for exams, interviews or anything else important. I used to think that by not preparing for speeches, my adrenalin and spontaneity would give it the edge I needed to make an impact. This is clearly rubbish – only an idiot would stand up in front of hundreds of people to deliver a 30-minute speech with just the bones of a structure. It was only after a bad performance that I took the advice of an excellent speaker – I started to prepare and practise my speeches. Not only do I feel relaxed as I'm totally prepared, I can confidently adlib as I always know where I can go back into my presentation. Result!

As per Day 27, your 'intention' is to find Mr Right – your 'method' must include always being prepared as you never know which corner he's going to appear from.

CASE STUDY

I met a client of mine for a coaching session. His hair was overdue for a cut, he was dressed in black shapeless clothes and an anorak and he hadn't shaved. When I asked why he hadn't made an effort with his appearance, he said that he wouldn't meet anyone special today. I was unaware that he had the gift of foresight or a crystal ball stashed away under his jacket. 'Suppose today you did meet someone?' I suggested. 'Are you looking as you would want them to see you?' He was horrified: 'Of course not!' He sat next to an attractive woman on the train home, but was so embarrassed by his appearance, he couldn't bring himself to talk to her – what a missed opportunity! Unless you have your own cast-iron method of fortune telling, always look how you want to be perceived.

Be prepared checklist

1 Always look your best – keep CSS at the top of your agenda.
2 Always have a lippy and a brush handy for remedial touch-ups.
3 Don't wander round frowning, wear a smile.
4 Always make the first non-verbal greeting with people you like the look of (smile, eyebrow flash – see Day 39).
5 Have a daily topical icebreaker using a positive perspective.

◉⟵ TOP TIP

- If you see the person regularly, as an ice-breaker ask them if they'd sponsor you for some worthy cause you support. You'll look interesting and it gives you the opportunity to chat to them again.

Activity

Increase your confidence in just 14 days

- Say each of the following positive affirmations 10 times each every day for the next two weeks.

- Look in the mirror while doing it, say it out loud, slowly, with a smile on your face – and mean it.

  – I am looking good.

  – I am positive.

  – I am interesting to new people.

  – I am ready for anything.

TAKE AN IN-DEPTH LOOK

How to spot every opportunity

There are other interest/opportunity-based options where you could meet Mr Right, although they have lower levels of single people and they're more challenging to crack. On the positive side, you'll get to meet new people and you'll learn a new thing or two – which will increase your confidence and stretch your comfort zone.

> **FACT:** The majority of people find their partners at work.

Activity

Where will you pull?

- Which area in your life have you been promising you'll do more of? Score the following statements from 1 to 5, 1 being 'Disagree strongly', 5 being 'Agree strongly'.

  – Learning something new. _____

  – Taking more exercise. _____

  – Reducing stress. _____

  – Increasing your circle of friends. _____

  – Getting out more. _____

- Choose the statement(s) with the highest score and compare it with the table opposite to find the activity that best suits your objectives.

- Move on to the day in Chapter 5 which applies to pulling in that area.

TAKE AN IN-DEPTH LOOK

Opportunities to meet people

	Pros	Cons
Commute to work	◆ You can practise it every day. ◆ Gives you something to do on the train/bus. ◆ Free.	◆ Difficult (but not impossible) in a car. ◆ If it doesn't work out you'll have to face them every day.
The gym	◆ Plenty of men there after work. ◆ Usually nice staff too. ◆ Exercise will keep you in shape and reduce your stress levels.	◆ May not look your best after a work-out. ◆ Limited opportunities for making 'the approach'.
Supermarket	◆ You have to go on a regular basis anyway. ◆ No entry charge. ◆ Easy to spot people shopping for one.	◆ Not a pulling zone – men don't have their 'single radar' on and may miss the obvious 'interest' signs.
Night classes	◆ You'll learn something new. ◆ Meet people with a common interest.	◆ Some classes have more men than others. ◆ Unlikely you'll pull on the first night.
Dance classes (salsa, ceroc, lindy hopping, etc.)	◆ Don't have to take a partner. ◆ You get to dance with everyone. ◆ Keeps you fit and reduces stress. ◆ More fun than the gym.	◆ Choice of class influences number of men. (Ballet/tap = 0 men) ◆ Difficult to get the right opportunity to make your move. ◆ Everyone is friendly, so the signs are sometimes overlooked.
Pubs/clubs	◆ Lots of people on the pull. ◆ Likely to pull on the night. ◆ Men are receptive to the signs. ◆ Getting dressed up and going out makes you feel great.	◆ Some clubs are like cattle markets. ◆ Be alert for drink spiking. ◆ Can be expensive. ◆ Some men are ritual pub/club-goers for womanising. ◆ Can be uncomfortable on your own.
Clubs	◆ Common interest with participants. ◆ Get to make new friends. ◆ Learn something new and increase your confidence.	◆ Some clubs attract more men than others (sugar craft = 0, Brazilian Juijitsu = lots of fit men under 35.)

TAKE AN IN-DEPTH LOOK

Your notes

CHAPTER 5

ALTERNATIVE DATING OPTIONS

Are you keeping up? Do you need some help? If you've not already subscribed, why not try the daily text messaging service for extra encouragement and support. Just text 'Settled 31' to 80881 now.

Each set of messages costs £1.50. Please see page x for full terms and conditions.

How to pull on the way to work

Your task for today is to break the commuting taboos. If you always travel at the same time you'll soon spot the familiar faces. Unfortunately there is an unwritten rule that we never make eye contact, exchange pleasantries or acknowledge our fellow commuters. It doesn't need to be that way!

The ground work

If you've seen someone you like, check out where they get on and off, or if they walk the same bit as you, where they work, etc. If they're reading something check it out, you can tell a lot about a person by what they read. Look for the absence of a wedding band.

Making the first move

Get them to notice you. Stand where you can see them and they can see you. When you catch their eye, give them an eyebrow flash. If they flash back that's a good sign. Next trip try smiling,

TOP TIP

◆ Take it more slowly when attracting a commuting prospect.

they'll recognise you from yesterday and should be happy to smile back.

Breaking the ice

Comment on an article in the paper they're reading:
◆ 'Do you know what's been happening in … (the latest reality TV programme)?'
◆ 'Could you tell me the price X company is trading at? I've just had a flutter on them.'
◆ 'Have you read the weather forecast for the weekend?'

If they're reading a book:
◆ 'I fancied that book, how are you finding it?'
◆ 'You seem riveted by that book, what's it about?'

ALTERNATIVE DATING OPTIONS

If they're not reading anything, compliment them on something:
◆ 'That's a great tie/watch/shoes/jacket, where did you get it? I'd like to get my brother/cousin one.'

Getting a date

Provided they've responded to your eyebrow flashes and smiles and are comfortable with your ice breaker, you can build the conversation up to their plans for the weekend. Ask them if they'd fancy meeting up for a coffee over the weekend or if they're free for a drink on the commute home.

TOP TIP

◆ The British love to talk about the weather, use it as a bridge to find out about their weekend plans.

CASE STUDY

Mel spotted a gorgeous guy at the university and was thrilled when she noticed him on her Metro home. She started by eyebrow flashing him, which he duly flashed back. Gradually, over the next few trips, she built it up to smiling, then turned it into a playful game of pulling tongues over the top of her paper. That day they chatted and arranged their first date.

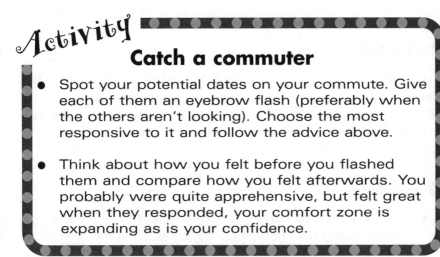

Activity
Catch a commuter

● Spot your potential dates on your commute. Give each of them an eyebrow flash (preferably when the others aren't looking). Choose the most responsive to it and follow the advice above.

● Think about how you felt before you flashed them and compare how you felt afterwards. You probably were quite apprehensive, but felt great when they responded, your comfort zone is expanding as is your confidence.

ALTERNATIVE DATING OPTIONS

How to pull at the gym

Trying to pull at the gym leaves you with a major dilemma. If you have a proper workout you may not be looking at your best – glowing fuchsia, with 'exercise hair' and sweat trickling down your face. However, staying pristine will seriously undermine the benefits you get from a good workout. I once asked a friend of mine how she always looked so glam whilst working out. She confessed that she came when it was quiet to do her hard work and just posed round the weight machines chatting to men during peak periods.

It's all well and good for ancient old Agony Aunts to recommend you pull down the gym – perhaps they should try it themselves first! On the plus side, you don't have to tread as carefully down the gym as you do on a commute, so be prepared to make a move as soon as you get the right signals.

The groundwork

Check out who's there on their own – men in twos are usually quite obsessed with their routine. Unless you're into narcissistic posers, you'll also want to avoid men covered in wet-look gel. Get close enough see if they're wearing a wedding band or have a white stripe if they've taken it off to exercise. See which bits of equipment they've used and if they've got a drink bottle with them. If they've not got a bottle they're going to have to use the water cooler at some stage so keep an eye out.

Making the first move

Get in a position where you can see them and they can see you. Give them an eyebrow flash. If they respond, give them a smile straight back. If they like you, they'll return the smile (if they're a bit shy, they may not smile, but you'll notice they keep catching your eye). On successful completion, move in.

TOP TIP

◆ If they don't respond to your eyebrow flash, try it a little closer. Some men don't wear their glasses in the gym.

Breaking the ice

Follow them on to a piece of equipment and:

◆ Say 'It's ages since I've used this piece, could you show me how to set it up please?'
◆ Talk about your routine and ask his advice on strength/stamina training (depending on whether he's spent more time on the cardiovascular machinery or the weights).

At the watercooler:

◆ Say 'Is it me or is it really hot in here?'
◆ Talk about your routine (as above).

Getting a date

If they've responded well to your conversation, move on to their plans for the weekend. Ask them if they fancy living a bit dangerously – there's a really hard class you fancy going to but don't want to go on your own. If they come with you, you can treat them to a coffee afterwards (provided it doesn't sabotage your image strategy). Alternatively, if they've got nothing planned see if they want to meet up for a workout and a refreshing juice afterwards.

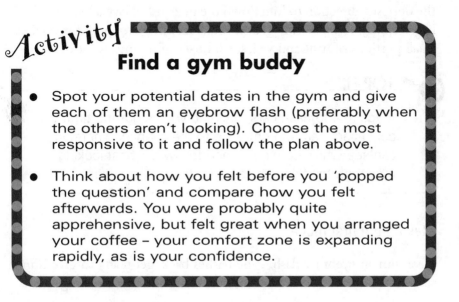

Activity

Find a gym buddy

● Spot your potential dates in the gym and give each of them an eyebrow flash (preferably when the others aren't looking). Choose the most responsive to it and follow the plan above.

● Think about how you felt before you 'popped the question' and compare how you felt afterwards. You were probably quite apprehensive, but felt great when you arranged your coffee – your comfort zone is expanding rapidly, as is your confidence.

ALTERNATIVE DATING OPTIONS

How to pull at the supermarket

Today, pulling whilst you're shopping. Most people navigate the supermarket on autopilot, so they're not as receptive to the signs as they would be in other situations. However, shopping is mind-numbingly boring, so see it as an opportunity to entertain yourself and possibly bag a man.

CASE STUDY

I did once date a man I met at Sainsburys. I was wearing hot pants and a bikini top (I'd been driving a tractor) at the time, so I caught the attention of virtually every shopper. Be attention grabbing if you want to snap people out of the monotony of shopping.

The groundwork

Make an effort and at least apply lippy. Follow the logical route round the store. Peruse the veg section and keep one eye out for men with baskets or shallow trollies. On spotting one you like the look of take the opposite direction to him down the next aisle. Have a look at what's in his trolley to make sure that it looks like he's shopping for one, i.e. small portions of fruit and veg, small boxes of tea, meals for one, etc.

TOP TIP

♦ If you're into flash cars, etc. and you've got the time you could park near the entrance to the car park where you can see who's coming in, and follow the best-looking men with the flashest cars into the supermarket.

Making the first move

Give him an eyebrow flash. If he flashes back, get ready to give him a smile in the next aisle. If he smiles back, move on to breaking the ice.

Breaking the ice

Take up a position next to him as he's selecting his next purchase. Catch his eye, then comment on something unusual in his trolley.

◆ 'What are those? I've never bought one as I wouldn't know what to do with it.'

If he only has TV dinners:

◆ 'I've heard that eating those is like trying to eat yourself to an early grave. Is it a convenience thing? If not the local restaurant is running cookery classes for busy professionals.'

Getting a date

If he responds positively, tell him that shopping really takes it out of you and ask if he fancies a quick pick-me-up coffee in the restaurant or drink in the bar across the road.

Activity

Flirt by the freezers

● Spot your potential dates in the supermarket and give each of them an eyebrow flash (preferably when the others aren't looking). Choose the most responsive to it and follow the plan above.

● Think about how you felt before you went shopping and compare how you felt afterwards. If you managed to pull first time, well done you! Whether you managed to find somebody or not, you've revolutionised a very dull necessity, and given your weekly shop a boost of adrenalin – plus you'll get the chance to practise again next week!

ALTERNATIVE DATING OPTIONS

How to pull at night classes

Today we're looking at the opportunity to expand your mind and meet Mr Right at the same time. You're going to be cocooned together for the next few weeks, so there's no need to strike straight away. Use the time to get to know your classmates better and to show them the best in you.

⊚ TOP TIP

♦ Pick subjects which are likely to have more men attending to increase your chances.

The groundwork

Get there early and eyebrow flash and smile at everyone as they walk in the door. They'll all gravitate to you as they look for someone to bond with and you'll appear the most popular girl in the class. Don't pick your seat, but hover around the teacher's desk until everyone's there, then choose the best spot.

Making the first move

If someone you like the look of arrives and sits down before the class starts, make a move to sit next to them. Otherwise wait until everyone starts to take their seat and ask the man of your choice if he minds if you sit next to him. Good manners and civility are the order of the day here. If he doesn't meet your expectations ensure you sit next to someone else next time and start the process again.

Breaking the ice

Get to understand their motivation for coming and build some empathy.

- 'What made you come to Spanish / car maintenance / webdesign / Italian cuisine?'
- 'How are you finding the course so far?'
- 'Do you have any other hobbies or interests?'

Make sure you mention that one of your reasons for coming is to meet some new people. If there's plenty of smiling and mirroring of body language (see Day 52), the rapport is good. If he appears to be single (i.e. he's not wearing a wedding ring or being picked up by his girlfriend afterwards), but he's not asked you out yet, then move on to getting a date.

Getting a date

Ask him at the beginning of the class if he fancies going for a coffee or a drink after the lesson. If he has plans ask if he wants to meet up next week. If he can't, and doesn't offer a reason, then take that as a polite refusal.

TOP TIP

- People are generally friendly at night classes – be sure you don't confuse the signals of someone being friendly with someone fancying you.

Activity **Back to school**

- Give every class member a warm welcome. Choose the one you most fancy and follow the plan above.

- Compare the feeling of trepidation you had prior to the class and the feeling after the class of being Miss Popular, as everyone is charmed and relieved by your friendly greeting. Your comfort zone is expanding as well as your IQ!

ALTERNATIVE DATING OPTIONS

How to pull at dance classes

Anyone who enjoyed dance classes as child will find the thought of returning an exciting and enjoyable prospect. Today we're going to look at pulling at a dance class. Most classes these days do not require you to attend with a partner – however, some have more male participants than others, and some dances are easier to master.

CASE STUDY

Patsy wanted to learn salsa, so she went to her local class and was thrilled to meet lots of new people. On the way home in the car, she noticed she was being followed by someone from the class. He explained he was too shy to make a move in front of the group and not quick enough to catch her in the car park, so he asked her to forgive him for taking the extreme move of following her. Within a few weeks Patsy had learned to salsa and moved in with her new man.

The groundwork

Leisure centres, bars and clubs are the most popular venues for dance lessons. Go along to all of them and check out which one has the most men and the best-looking attendees. Check for wedding bands prior to making the first move.

TOP TIP

+ Choose a class where you automatically get moved round the other dancers, rather than one where you're partnered up.

Making the first move

By being in an embrace you've already broken the physiological barrier – all you have to do is show him that you're interested. You don't get much of a chance to chat whilst you're dancing as all your energy goes on learning the steps. Give him a friendly smile and lots of eye contact to let him know you're interested. If he responds in kind, break the ice.

Breaking the ice

Ask:

- 'I'm new to this, how do you think I'm doing?'
- 'Have you been coming here long?'
- 'Do you go to any other dance classes?'
- 'Do you come with anyone?'

This will get the conversation going and will help to identify whether he has a girlfriend/wife. If his facial language is friendly and he asks questions in return, take this as a positive sign.

Getting a date

Comment what thirsty work learning to dance is and ask if he'd like to go for a drink afterwards. If he already has commitments, see if he'd be free before or after class the following week.

Activity **Dance partners**

- Once you've chosen your class, turn up assuming the CSS stance (see Day 27) and follow the steps above.

- Compare the feeling of trepidation you had prior to the class and the feeling after the class of having made a physical connection with other people. Your comfort zone and confidence is expanding as well as your level of fitness!

ALTERNATIVE DATING OPTIONS

How to pull at pubs and clubs

Being from the North East, I learned most of my flirting tricks down the Quayside in Newcastle, which is not only one of the best nights out in Europe, it's also the friendliest. The best part of a night out is the anticipation, getting yourself looking gorgeous and looking forward to letting your hair down. If you pull on top of that, it's just a bonus. If clubbing isn't your thing, pick a casino instead. The other advantage of this activity is that it's likely to have a higher proliferation of single men.

The groundwork

The bigger the town or city, the more choice you have in terms of diversity of venues. Pick a girlfriend who has similar tastes in music and men to you and prepare for the night out. The local 'What's on' magazine will have all the latest venues, as will the internet.

TOP TIP

◆ Ask round at work for recommendations for a night out.

Making the first move

Find yourself a spot where you can see and be seen. Men on the pull will usually be scanning the room. Once you've spotted someone you like:

1 Make eye contact for 4 seconds.
2 Drop your eyes then look back.
3 If he's still looking give him a smile.
4 If he smiles back, you're in.

Breaking the ice

Men generally accept that they have to do the running in these situations, but he'll be chuffed to bits if you take the initiative. Ask:

♦ 'We're just here for the night – can you recommend where else is worth trying?'

If he's interested he'll use the excuse to chat further to you.

Alternatively, use your girlfriend as a decoy and push her (gently) into the man concerned. Say:

♦ 'I must apologise for my girlfriend! She's not normally like this – we're celebrating.'

If he's interested he'll empathise with you and ask more about what you're celebrating.

Getting a date

If you'd like to see him again say:

♦ 'I've really enjoyed meeting you, I'd like to meet up for a drink sometime – if you fancy it. Here's my number – give me a call next week and we can fix something up.'

If you've arranged a date, make sure you get his number to reconfirm nearer the time.

TOP TIP

♦ Only accept a drink if:
  – You can see it being poured.
  – It's handed straight to you.
  – You can keep it with you.

Activity

Out on the pull

● Once you've fixed a date with your girlfriend follow the steps above.

● Compare the feeling of anticipation you had prior to your night out and the feeling afterwards (hopefully not too hungover). Your comfort zone and confidence are expanding, as well as your social activities!

ALTERNATIVE DATING OPTIONS

How to pull at societies and clubs

Today we're looking at pulling at clubs of the social variety. Your interests or occupation will have a large bearing on which would be the most appropriate clubs for you to join. These in turn will have less or more men in your age range, dependant on your selection.

The groundwork

Find the sort of clubs you are interested in either on the internet, in the local paper or at the library. Contact the organiser prior to going to check the demographic of the group and the types of activities they cover. If you think it's the right club for you ask if they'll chaperone you round at the next meeting. Keep an eye out for wedding bands.

Making the first move

It's not a dating event, so don't expect to pull on the first night. Take advantage of the time to get to know people better. The first person who catches your eye may not necessarily be the one who's best suited to you. When you feel there's someone you particularly like, let them know by spending more time with them and giving them slightly longer eye contact and lots of smiles. If they reciprocate it's positive but not conclusive. It's expected to ask basic questions like what do they do, where do they work, have they been doing this long, etc.

TOP TIP

- ◆ Try these useful links for some ideas:
  - Brazilian Jui Jitsu (BJJ) www.sfuk.net
  - Toastmasters www.the-asc.org.uk
  - Rileys Snooker and Pool www.fcsnooker.co.uk
  - Writers Guild www.writersguild.org.uk

ALTERNATIVE DATING OPTIONS

Breaking the ice

Say:

- 'I'm new to this area and I'd really like to check out the bar/café. Would you like to join me to check it out with a pre-event bite to eat / post-event drink?'
- 'I've got to visit a client who works near your offices. Do you fancy meeting up for coffee next Friday lunchtime?'

Getting the date

When you're on your own, see if he reacts in the same way or if he's more flirtatious. Move things up a notch by mirroring his actions and get in closer proximity to him (see Day 46). If he responds in kind, it's likely that he'll make the next move to a proper date. If not, take the initiative:

- 'I've really enjoyed spending time with you. If you'd like to do it again, here's my number – give me a call.'

Activity
Join a club

- Choose which of the following areas interest you most then follow the steps above.
  - **Learning something for work** Toastmasters, web design, etc.
  - **Keeping fit** Brazilian Jui Jitsu, rock climbing, canoeing, etc.
  - **Doing something sociable** Join a pool hall (e.g. Rileys), chess club, writers club, etc.

- Consider not only how your comfort zone was expanded by meeting new people, but also how you were challenged physically and mentally by the activity itself. Congratulate yourself on your efforts – you should be feeling energised by doing something new and proud of yourself for being proactive.

ALTERNATIVE DATING OPTIONS

Your notes

CHAPTER 6

BODY LANGUAGE TO GET YOU NOTICED

How to get yourself noticed

Over the next few days we're going to master the all the basics to get you noticed and give off the right signals. These lessons are vital for every encounter you'll have, so study them well. Positioning is the first vital tip.

Being a wall flower or standing where nobody can see you will seriously reduce the number of opportunities available to you.

TOP TIP

◆ People are more likely to approach you if they've seen you.

It's a comfort zone always to stand or sit where you're used to – for example, the same seat on the bus, the same spot in the car park, the same seat in a meeting, the spot at the quiet end of the bar, etc.

To maximise your chances of meeting more people and giving yourself maximum exposure, study the lists below.

Optimum positioning

The best places to be are:

◆ In the busiest part of the room
◆ Where you are in full view of people entering the room
◆ An aisle seat on the commute to work
◆ The middle seats on a table with the best view of the room and the door
◆ At the centre or the busiest part of a bar
◆ Move car parking spots at work next to a man that you find attractive, he'll probably park there each day out of habit.

Getting noticed

1 Stand up tall (see Day 40).
2 Make sure you make eye contact with anyone who looks your way (see Day 39).
3 If you like the look of them, give them a friendly, closed-lip smile.

Activity

Pole position

● Make a mental note when you're around people of where would be the best place to stand for maximum exposure. Move into that point. If that's not possible, make sure the next time you're in that situation that you gain the best spot.

● Compare how many more opportunities there are, and how much more eye contact you make, in your new optimum positioning.

● Be confident and savour the increased attention you receive.

BODY LANGUAGE TO GET YOU NOTICED

How to make all-important eye contact

'The eyes are the window to the soul.' Proverb

Eye contact is the very first non-verbal clue that you've acknowledged someone. It's the best way of saying a myriad of things without committing or embarrassing yourself, or even opening your mouth.

Some people feel uncomfortable making eye contact for all sorts of reasons. To fix this, try looking into someone's eyes for as long as you're comfortable, then look at the top of their head, then bring your eyes back

> **TOP TIP**
>
> ◆ Never approach somebody you haven't made eye contact with first.

to theirs again, and so on. Gradually increase the length of time you look into their eyes until you're making good eye contact all the time. Alternatively, you could look at the bridge of their nose – from a distance they won't be able to tell you're not looking them in the eye, but beware, up close you can appear a little cock-eyed!

If you already possess good eye contact make more use of it to promote better liking of yourself and more positive responses from other people.

1 Getting eye contact

Look in their direction – people usually instinctively know they're being watched and they should look your way.

> **FACT:** People like people with dilated pupils more than contracted ones. Hence don't stand with a bright light in your eyes shrinking them!

2 The eyebrow flash

This is a universally accepted welcome gesture. Simply raise your eyebrows quickly up and down, once. Most people mirror your gesture without even thinking and will eyebrow flash you back. This can break down a barrier in that they have inadvertently acknowledged you with a positive gesture.

- Don't stare for longer than 10 seconds. It's a sign of aggression.

3 Catching attention

Keep their eye contact for 4 seconds, look away or drop your eyes – then look back. If they're still looking, they're interested. Give them a smile, or play with them a bit by obscuring your face behind a glass or a menu. Catch their eye again for 4 seconds and repeat. If they smile back, you've virtually said hello, I quite like the look of you and the feeling is mutual.

4 Sexing up contact

Give them a long, slow blink with a lips-closed smile. Not only does it look sexy, it'll leave them in no doubt that they're the centre of your attention.

Mastering good eye contact will give you increased confidence in every aspect of your life, from professional to personal. It's an underrated but essential skill to conquer.

Activity

Make more eye contact

- Firstly, look at the everyday interactions you have with people. Build up the amount of eye contact you're making on a professional and friendly level. Enjoy how people react positively to it.

- Now try it more with strangers, using steps 1 and 2. Build it up to steps 3 and 4 on men you find attractive.

BODY LANGUAGE TO GET YOU NOTICED

Mastering walking tall

A person's posture says a lot about them. If you're all hunched over people may interpret it as a lack of confidence or self-esteem. Conversely, someone who walks tall with their head held high appears confident and more approachable. You want your posture to say the right things about you.

CASE STUDY

Jen was lacking in height and thought some killer heels would do the trick. Unfortunately they had the opposite effect, as she ended doubled over trying to walk in them. She tried less of a heel and took smaller steps – the effect was perfect, with more height, less speed and far more sophistication.

Stance

Imagine you're naked in front of the man of your dreams. You'd suck your stomach in, tuck your bottom under and make yourself as tall and streamlined as you could. This is the pose you should always try to adopt.

The walk

As a rule of thumb, the higher the heel, the smaller the step you should make. Walk from the hip, not the knee, for maximum elegance.

TOP TIP

♦ Walking more slowly will give people more opportunity to notice you.

DAY 40: MASTERING WALKING TALL

To give your walk more interest and to be more eye-catching, imagine you're walking along a tightrope on the ground – each foot should be placed in a midline with the other following in front of it. Swing your opposite arm gently when you walk – it'll give you a natural wiggle.

⊙⚡ TOP TIP

- ◆ Wearing heels will give your calves a better shape, tighten your legs and give your bottom 30% more protrusion.

Activity
Walk tall

- Whether you're a yomper or a skulker, get into the habit of walking properly. If you can, get a friend to video you walking. It's incredibly difficult to walk on camera, so don't be surprised if it takes a couple of goes to capture it. Now practise walking tall and film that. Play the two clips back and compare the eye-catching difference.

- Arrange for someone you trust to tell you when you've reverted back to your old habits to keep your 'walking tall' on track.

BODY LANGUAGE TO GET YOU NOTICED

91

Are you keeping up? Do you need some help? If you've not already subscribed, why not try the daily text messaging service for extra encouragement and support. Just text 'Settled 41' to 80881 now.

Each set of messages costs £1.50. Please see page x for full terms and conditions.

Get perfect posture – sitting pretty

Men are attracted to colour and shape. You can make yourself very shapely when you sit and can draw attention just by the way you're postured.

The Queen and Mrs Thatcher look regal when they sit, Gwen Stefani and Pink look dirty, Liz Hurley looks graceful, Madonna looks domineering, Catherine Zeta-Jones oozes star quality and Mrs Overall from Acorn antiques just looks gnarled.

TOP TIP

◆ Having a sitting posture different from the people around you will make you stand out.

One of the most clichéd but effective pulling sitting positions is with your legs crossed at the knees and the shoe dangling from the gently flexing toes of the foot that's off the floor. (It goes without saying that it has more impact with a strappy sandal than a trainer.) Try it once you've caught the eye of someone you find attractive.

There are others:

The willow If you're long-limbed and lithe, you can pull this one off. Sit with your legs wrapped round each other, arms intertwined and spine relaxed in a gentle curve.

The perch If you're shorter or bustier, sit towards the front of the seat, cross your legs at the ankles, and keep your back straight and your chest out.

The slouch (in trousers) Lean right back in your seat with your feet hip distance apart and your knees relaxed open. Rest your hands on your hip bones (not crossed) and play freely, in big movements, with your hair.

TOP TIP

- To look and feel relaxed, don't fold your arms under your chest.

Activity How to sit

- Next time you're in a café, notice the posture of the other customers. Are they slouched in their chairs, tucked under the tables, resting their head in their hands? Make a list of who stands out. What do you notice about their body language? Which of the positions above does it match?

- When you're out with friends, experiment with your sitting position to see which is the most comfortable for you and which gives the most eye-catching position. Adopt it always.

BODY LANGUAGE TO GET YOU NOTICED

Are you making a star entrance?

Whenever I'm approached it's usually accompanied by the comment, 'I noticed you as soon as you walked into the room.' I can guarantee that whether it's work or social, if I'm going somewhere alone I won't be on my own for very long.

FACT: 80% of people will have made a snap decision about you by the time you've moved from one side of the room to the other.

You can get ahead of the game in the first impressions stake by getting others to notice you before you've even clapped eyes on them.

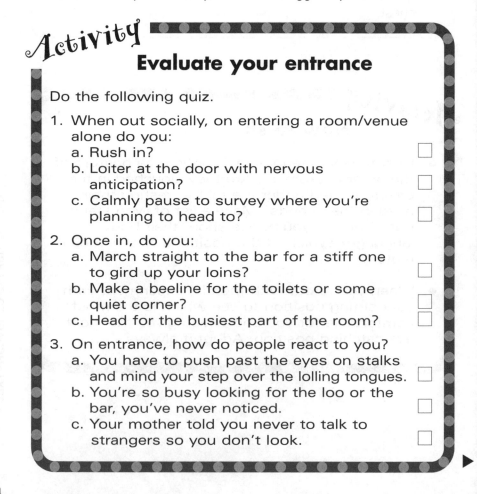

Activity

Evaluate your entrance

Do the following quiz.

1. When out socially, on entering a room/venue alone do you:
   a. Rush in? ☐
   b. Loiter at the door with nervous anticipation? ☐
   c. Calmly pause to survey where you're planning to head to? ☐

2. Once in, do you:
   a. March straight to the bar for a stiff one to gird up your loins? ☐
   b. Make a beeline for the toilets or some quiet corner? ☐
   c. Head for the busiest part of the room? ☐

3. On entrance, how do people react to you?
   a. You have to push past the eyes on stalks and mind your step over the lolling tongues. ☐
   b. You're so busy looking for the loo or the bar, you've never noticed. ☐
   c. Your mother told you never to talk to strangers so you don't look. ☐

▶

4. If you were to liken your entrance to one of the following, whom would it be?
   a. Dot Cotton
   b. Jessica Rabbit
   c. Bridget Jones

5. Once settled in the room do you find that you usually end up facing:
   a. The wall?
   b. The main part of the room?
   c. Don't recall which direction you face.

Tot up your scores to see how you've fared.

1. a) 2   b) 3   c) 1
2. a) 2   b) 3   c) 1
3. a) 1   b) 2   c) 3
4. a) 3   b) 1   c) 2
5. a) 2   b) 1   c) 3

If you scored:

Under 7 You've either got an ego the size of Brazil or you're blessed. Either way we can use this to your advantage to hone your skills and make your entrance truly stunning. Get some people who know you well to mark you on the quiz. Are the scores still matching up? If your answers haven't married up with those of your friends, accept their feedback graciously. It's good to see the positive in a situation but not to the extent that it's giving you an unrealistic outlook on yourself and your behaviour. This is a major barrier to achieving your *Single to settled* goal, so make a note to view things with a more unbiased perspective.

Between 7 and 11 Your entrance is average to middling and you need to pay attention to the factors in giving off a confident vibe to maximise your first impressions.

Over 12 Not only are you uncomfortable in your surroundings, you are unaware of what's going on around you and what you should be paying attention to. But not to worry – you'll be demonstrating the biggest improvement of all the scores when you've finished this section.

BODY LANGUAGE TO GET YOU NOTICED

Making a stunning entrance

Every day you get numerous opportunities to make an entrance – don't waste any of them. Mr Right, his best friend or his brother could be on the other side of the door you're walking through.

When I was the Flirting Expert for *Sex and the City*, I had to watch a whole series prior to the DVD release. One thing they did consistently well was make a fabulous entrance. If you're in any doubt how to do it brilliantly, have a watch.

Entrance

Before walking in, make sure that you're not going to get lost in a crowd. Move to the side and let them pass.

Pause

As you walk through the entrance to the main room, pause for a moment.

Smile

Look at the busiest part of the room and give it a broad smile (as if you've seen someone you recognise). Anyone who's single will generally have one eye on the door and they're bound to spot you with your confident entrance and friendly attitude. Don't feel foolish about smiling at strangers, they'll just assume you're smiling at someone else around them.

TOP TIP

♦ Before entering:
  – Adjust your attire
  – Assume the naked stance
  – Take a deep breath and smile.

BODY LANGUAGE TO GET YOU NOTICED

Parade

If there are stairs, do a very slow, sassy walk down them.

TOP TIP

◆ Don't:
  – Enter at the same time as a crowd
  – Sneak straight to the bar/ loo
  – Rush.

Instead of rushing straight to the bar, parade through the busiest part of the room to make sure everyone gets a chance to see you at your best first.

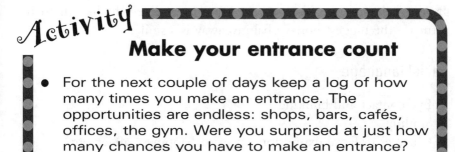

Activity

Make your entrance count

● For the next couple of days keep a log of how many times you make an entrance. The opportunities are endless: shops, bars, cafés, offices, the gym. Were you surprised at just how many chances you have to make an entrance?

● Practise the 'entrance – pause – smile – parade' technique on a reduced scale every time you have to make an entrance.

● Once you get the hang of the sequence, arrange to go out with a girlfriend to a part of town with plenty of bars. Have fun in each one making a double-act *Sex and the City* entrance for twice the impact.

● Consider how much easier you find it walking into a room full of strangers with this eye-catching new entrance.

BODY LANGUAGE TO GET YOU NOTICED

It's all in your expression

With statistics like this, facial language is obviously the area to focus on as likely to have the biggest impact when you first meet your man. Facial language is basically the expression and animation in your face.

> **FACT:** Facial language accounts for 40% of the body language absorbed in a first encounter.

People who have good facial expression:

◆ Are easy to read
◆ Look interesting
◆ Feel easy to engage.

If you feel someone likes you, you are more likely to like them in return – the biggest non-verbal giveaway is a smile.

Facial language

◆ Eye contact and blinking
◆ Smiling
◆ Changes in facial expression (surprise, happiness, anger, etc.)
◆ Head movements (nodding in agreement and tilting when listening)
◆ Eyebrow raises and flashes
◆ Nose-wrinkling (being playful or in objection).

We've all watched someone being interviewed on TV who is stony-faced, i.e. without movement. They generally don't leave you with a good impression of them. However, the person who engages in eye contact, tilts their head whilst listening, smiles freely and changes expression with the twists and turns of the conversation, will leave a positive impression. By increasing the animation in your face the person you're with thinks you're interested in them and their conversation – you'll be amazed at the results.

Activity

Focus on your facial expressions

- Either in the office or socially, the next time you speak with a good friend or associate, use no facial expressions. Observe how they react – does the conversation get awkward and end prematurely, or does it flow like it normally does?

- Now try it with a relative stranger, but this time use more facial language than you would normally. Does the conversation flow better, are they reacting more positively to you than a stranger would normally? How do you feel about it (maybe a little silly or odd at first)? You will gradually feel more confident in your ability to engage strangers.

- Make a mental note to focus on your facial language for the rest of this book until it becomes a good habit.

BODY LANGUAGE TO GET YOU NOTICED

How to issue a silent invitation

You may be wondering when we're actually going to get on to making that unjustly feared approach. What a lot of people fail to recognise is that by getting all the non-verbal gestures right in advance and looking for the appropriate reactions, you're maximising your chances of success and minimising your chances of rejection, plus giving your confidence a massive boost along the way.

In Day 43 we made our stunning entrance, giving everyone an opportunity to preview us; on Day 39 we perfected that first eye contact. Now we're going to add this to yesterday's facial language to make a distinctive and unmissable hello in any language.

You'll use this technique in a situation where you can't speak to your man or he's too far away:

◆ Make eye contact for 4 seconds, drop your gaze and look back to test if you've got his attention. If he's still looking do it again.

◆ Give him a slight smile with an eyebrow raise. He should flash you back.

◆ Give your hair a slow but reassuring plump with a biggish arm gesture (provided it's not full of product or in a style that won't take a preening). If you look in his direction he should be watching you. Give him another smile.

You'll now be animated enough for him to watch you out of curiosity. I enjoy playing a little mirroring game with my facial expression and head tilts and nods. I even do it with children either in cars or supermarket trolleys – it gets a fantastic reaction every time. If, however, you don't feel like a game of facial gymnastics, use a simple but pronounced gesture to get him to act.

Either tilt your head in the direction you want him to move (i.e. to the bar) then look in the same direction, before reconnecting eye contact and nodding once. He will return your nod, at which point you should start to walk immediately (and nakedly) towards the bar.

Or shake your glass in front of your face and tilt your head towards it whilst raising your eyebrows. Can be interpreted as 'Fancy a drink?' or 'Can I get you a drink?' Again start to walk towards the bar.

When the initial responses have been positive, I've **never** seen a man decline this invitation to join a woman.

TOP TIP

◆ Most men find approaching women so confusing and nerve-racking that they'll be delighted you took the initiative.

Issue some invitations

● Treat yourself to a night out with a friend. Make a game out of how many men's eyes you can catch and to what stage you can take them in the task above.

● Observe which factors influence your outcomes. Does greater animation give better results? Is there an optimum distance that works best for you? Do you get more hits from men who have caught your eye first, etc?

● How do you feel about completing the task. Can you feel your confidence and comfort zone being tested and expanded every day?

BODY LANGUAGE TO GET YOU NOTICED

How to get in his space effortlessly

To keep a man at his ease and to stop you looking overly keen, you need to hit his personal space at just the right distance. If you come from a small town your personal space is likely to be larger than someone from a city who is used to a diminished personal space. Personal space is also different for different nationalities (a Briton tends to like more space than a Brazilian). The end result of having your space invaded is a feeling of discomfort and unease.

The zones

The public zone, 3 m plus This is the space you'll be making initial eye contact from.

The social consultative zone, 1.2–3 m Everyday social and business encounters, chatting in groups, etc.

The personal zone, 0.5–1.2 m Arms length from each other, able to shake hands.

The intimate zone, 0–0.5 m Where you are ultimately aiming for – you are touching or are able to touch easily.

TOP TIP

♦ Approach him from the front, or a place where you can make eye contact prior to getting in his space.

You're now ready to approach him, following your non-verbal invitation to join you (Day 45). Good manners and civility cost nothing and are appreciated by everyone. Rather than invading his space, ask to be invited in first. Say 'Hi, do you mind if I join you?' He's going to say 'Yes', at which point you can move into the outer limits of his personal zone.

You've crashed his zone if he:

♦ Bobs his head backwards
♦ Leans backwards
♦ Takes a step back.

In which case, take a small step backwards to make him more at ease.

As the conversation builds and you spot the signs that he likes you (see Day 52), you'll probably intuitively move closer.

TOP TIP

- Build up touching from a one-second light hand-to-arm touch to a lingering touch when you're in each other's intimate zone.
- Go for upper-body non-erogenous zones.
- Don't paw. Don't touch him if he pulls away.

Once body contact has been established and you're touching freely, you can manoeuvre him into a full-body alignment position in his intimate zone. By full-body alignment we mean that toes, knees, hips and shoulders are all parallel to each other. It's an extremely powerful position and not one you enter into on a daily basis with just anyone. Check for 'crashing zones' signs. With this power move you can get his number, get a date or head in for a kiss (if he's not gone for you first).

Activity

Personal space

- At work or with a friend, try standing much closer to someone than you would normally and observe what happens. They'll probably either lean backwards or take a step away – they may even terminate the conversation prematurely.

- If there's someone you've fancied for a while, when you're in a more social setting try manoeuvring into the inner boundaries of their personal zone, then gradually work their intimate zone. Can you effect a full-body alignment?

- How do you feel getting into someone else's space? Was it easy? Is it getting easier with practise?

BODY LANGUAGE TO GET YOU NOTICED

Your notes

....

....

....

....

....

....

....

....

....

....

....

....

....

....

....

CHAPTER 7

THE ART OF
CONVERSATION

Breaking the ice like a pro

Breaking the ice doesn't have to be tough, especially if you've used the non-verbal 'Hellos' covered in the previous few days. However, learned experience tells us that it's difficult. Today we're going to dispel that myth.

You may open a conversation by asking permission: 'Hi! May I join you?' (as in Day 46). If not, another good way for women to start a conversation is with a compliment. People are much more likely to like you if they think you like them. (I've mentioned this already – it's a key point in building relationships.) If you are gifted at joke-telling (and the vast majority aren't) you could open with a gag – but don't be tempted to tell endless jokes, as the other person will find it difficult to get to know you and it makes it very hard to have a conversation. If you're not a natural comedian, don't waste your time or nervous energy trying to pull off a complex chat-up line or joke. You could plump for a standard opener: 'Are you out with friends?' 'It's nice here, isn't it?' 'How do you know the host?' But my favourite is the simple but genuine compliment.

Base the compliment on what first attracted you to them, or on something interesting about them.

- 'You have the biggest smile.'
- 'I'm a sucker for big, brown eyes.'
- 'You really suit that shirt/aftershave.'
- 'I really love your accent.'

TOP TIP

When giving compliments:
- Keep it short.
- Be genuine.
- Deliver it with eye contact.

The compliment doesn't have to be long, convoluted or complex. Keep it simple for maximum effect.

It's not just what you say but how you say it. Brits can be terribly conservative – if you mumble a compliment your target may think you're being insincere, which is worse than not giving one in the first place. Say it like you mean it and with good eye contact.

It sounds basic, maybe even a bit corny, but it's fabulously effective.

TOP TIP

◆ Learn to accept a compliment. 'Thank you' is fine as an acceptance.

Activity

Get confident with compliments

● Practise genuine compliments on the people around you, male and female. Don't just use compliments that refer to their appearance – compliment them on the way they've done a job for you. 'Well done on that task, you've done it brilliantly.' 'Thanks for doing that for me, that's really kind of you.' 'I really admire the way you tackle things so positively,' etc.

● How do they react to you? Do they look pleased?

● Once you're confident at dishing out compliments and have experienced the great benefits of it, direct your compliments at someone you're attracted to.

● How do they react?

● How do you feel? More confident/bolder/ pleased?

THE ART OF CONVERSATION

How to make killer conversation

It's a common concern that you will 'dry up' in conversation. Men worry about this more because they aren't as skilled as women at small talk. Also they feel the pressure is more on

TOP TIP

♦ Aim to be interested rather than interesting.

them to make the conversation, as men generally are expected to do the running. Therefore any effort on your part is gratefully accepted by your relieved male recipient.

The best conversations are when:

♦ You listen attentively to the other person
♦ You look interested in what they're saying
♦ You find common ground to talk about.

CASE STUDY

John's first date could talk the legs off a table and he couldn't get a word in edgeways. However, his next date was perfect – she was great company and very interesting. On further investigation he realised he hadn't learned that much about her. She'd listened attentively to him and built on his conversation, leaving him feeling good about himself – and her.

Use open questions, i.e. ones that don't lead to a 'Yes' or 'No' answer. These usually start with 'who', 'when', 'what', 'where', 'how' or 'why'. Find which common ground you share and build on from there.

♦ 'What brought you here tonight?'
♦ 'How do you know the host?'
♦ 'Where are you headed off to next?'
♦ 'How does this compare to your usual watering hole?'

THE ART OF CONVERSATION

DAY 48: HOW TO MAKE KILLER CONVERSATION

DON'TS

Never:

◆ Talk about your ex
◆ Outdo his stories
◆ Domineer or hijack the conversation
◆ Put yourself down at the end of sentences
◆ Be negative.

Conversation topics

◆ Be sure you're up to date on the day's news. Ask his opinion on the latest stories, it'll give you an idea of what makes him tick.
◆ Ask about any holidays he's got booked and where he likes to travel.
◆ Ask if there's anything exciting he's got coming up.
◆ Ask about his work (but don't be a work bore).

TOP TIP

◆ Maintain eye contact whilst he speaks.

Activity
Become a better conversationist

● Have a conversation with your friends during which they note down each time you draw attention to your flaws. Are you surprised by how many times you did it?

● If so, monitor all your own conversations the next day and see how it affects work and your other relationships.

● Practise making conversation with strangers, for example at the coffee stand at the station.

● By now you're reaping the results of your earlier dating activities, so try it on with someone you find attractive and see how much longer you can keep the conversation going.

THE ART OF CONVERSATION

What's the measure of your conversation?

By now your comfort zone has been stretched and resized to include flirting with strangers, approaching strangers, dishing out compliments and chatting away confidently. You should be feeling very proud of yourself for the progress you've made. However, it would be useful to know how your charms are being received.

There is a cunning tool called the IIC (Impersonal Interrogative Comment) formula which will let you judge how keen someone is to continue talking to you. It can be used in most contexts, social or business, provided the question is geared to provoke a response, i.e. with a simple rising question at the end.

What you're looking for in their response is:

◆ Length
◆ Personalising
◆ Questioning.

I have a necklace with a cat face on it. I don't particularly like cats, but I can guarantee people will comment on it when I wear it. They usually ask 'Do you like cats?'

Negative

If I'm not interested in talking they get a straight 'No'. The **length** is shorter than the original question, signifying that I don't wish to continue the conversation.

Neutral

If I'm OK about talking to them I say, 'Not really, it's just an eye-catching necklace.' The **length** is about the same length as their original question, indicating that I'm fine talking to them.

Positive

If I like them I say, 'Not really, I just liked the design – it's quite unusual and most people comment on it.' The **length** is longer and I've used **personalisation** in it (the word 'I'). These are two good clues that I want to continue the conversation.

Best

If it's someone I really want to talk to I say, 'I love cats but I had to give mine away due to an allergy. Do you have a cat?' The **length** is longer, I've **personalised** it with 'I' and 'you' and I'm **questioning** at the end, inviting a response from them and encouraging further dialogue.

Activity

Have the best conversations

- At work or with new acquaintances, look for length, personalising and questioning in their responses to your questions. You won't be surprised to see that it's the people you're most friendly with that give the **Best** ranking with this formula.

- With one of your potential dates, try improving your responses to their questions by incorporating more length, personalising and questioning. Note what happens to the quality of your conversation. Do you find that asking questions and inviting more responses leads to a longer, more positive conversation?

THE ART OF CONVERSATION

Are you lowering the tone?

I've been accused of being able to drag any conversation into the gutter, but that's not what we're referring to here. Tonality accounts for 23% of the overall impression you give when you first meet someone. Your tonality is the pitch and modulation in your voice.

CASE STUDY

I was interviewed recently by a newsreader whom I didn't care for, having seeing her on the TV. Her static pitch and clipped delivery made her seem aloof and uninterested in her interviewees. In real life she couldn't have been more different – she had a lovely intonation and, although she used the same language, the way she said it made her appear much more friendly. On hearing her off-camera voice I warmed to her straight away.

Take care to avoid the following voice problems:

Too quiet People will tire of having to listen intently to catch what you're saying and you may appear depressed.

Monotone You'll sound dull and uninteresting regardless of how fascinating your topic of conversation.

Very clipped and quick You'll sound rushed and uninterested.

Loud and booming with too much variation You'll sound bombastic and full of yourself.

The perfect tonality has:

◆ Enough volume to be heard comfortably in your surroundings
◆ Appropriate variation of pitch and pace
◆ Good, rounded tone.

A combination of these three factors will keep your companion's interest. As with mirroring body language, mirroring verbal language is also powerful. Use some of the phrases and terminology he uses to literally talk the same language – it builds rapport quickly and he'll feel a common ground with you.

It's not what you say but how you say it that will cause the most impact. One word said with differing intonation can convey anything from agreement to lust! If you say 'Coffee?' quickly and abruptly it's an enquiry as to whether they'd like a cup. If you say it softer, slightly lower and drawn out with a rising intonation at the end, it can be pure seduction.

Activity

Tinker with your tone

- Tonality is just as powerful as full-body alignment – by lowering your tone you can change the atmosphere in an instant. To practise, try using a different pitch and intonation when giving one-word answers to colleagues and friends. 'Yes' and 'No' are easy words to choose. Use them to provoke further response or to kill the conversation. How did you find this and how effective was it for you?

- When you're well into conversation with your date, play with the tonality of your voice. Make it slower and softer when you lean in to talk to him – he'll have to lean closer to hear then, all of a sudden, you have an intimate tête-à-tête.

THE ART OF CONVERSATION

Are you keeping up? Do you need some help? If you've not already subscribed, why not try the daily text messaging service for extra encouragement and support. Just text 'Settled 51' to 80881 now.

Each set of messages costs £1.50. Please see page x for full terms and conditions.

How to close the conversation

'Good manners cost nothing.'

Once you've mastered the art of getting anyone to talk to you, you have to learn the trick of ending it. There's no need to hang around in a conversation for longer than is necessary to arrange your first date. If he gets your life story at your initial meeting it doesn't leave a lot for future encounters.

When to move on

◆ When gaps and lulls appear in the conversation
◆ When you've arranged your date
◆ If you decide you don't fancy him
◆ Your gut feeling tells you something isn't right.

Bad gut feeling

Always trust your instincts. Tell him you promised to meet up with friends and you'll have to call them. Make sure that somebody knows where you are and arrange to contact them again once you're safely away.

TOP TIP

◆ If you don't want to give him your number, say you've just got a new number which you can't remember and ask for his instead.

What to do

Park them on someone else

Take the opportunity to introduce him to someone you know. Get a conversation going ('Jim was just telling me about sky diving. Jim – tell Fran all about it, she's really interested in that sort of thing.') then make your excuses and leave.

THE ART OF CONVERSATION

Let them go

Simply say, 'It's been interesting chatting to you. I've taken up a lot of your time and must let you get back to what you were doing.'

Close after the date's arranged

Say, 'It's been great meeting you, I'm really looking forward to seeing you on the 6th. I'd better let you get back to your mates and rescue my friend – she's been abandoned for the last hour.'

TOP TIP

- Don't sneak to the loo – he may be there waiting when you come out.
- Don't peer over his shoulder trying to catch the eye of someone more interesting.
- Don't be rude.
- Don't give him your number just to get rid of him.

Activity

Take control – close the conversation

- There's always someone at work or socially whom it's difficult to get rid of once you're stuck with them. Instead of suffering them or avoiding them altogether, try parking them with other colleagues or friends.

- Monitor the conversations you're having with your potential dates. Do you let them run thin before you finish them? Do you always leave it to them to finish the conversation? Do you wish you had more control over when to end it?

- Identify which problem affects you most and practise ending the conversation in those circumstances. How do you feel when you're controlling the close of the conversation? Liberated, relieved, in control?

THE ART OF CONVERSATION

Your notes

CHAPTER 8

IS LOVE IN THE AIR?

How can I tell if he fancies me?

It's unusual for a man to declare how much he likes you in the early stages. One of the easiest ways to find out is to piece together all the clues you've had to date from his body language.

Eyeline triangle

When you first meet a man who likes you he may do an eyeline triangle. This is where his eyes go down from yours, then back up again. Generally the bigger the triangle the more he likes you. If he triangles to your mouth – he's quite interested; chest – more interested; looking you all the way up and down – very interested. It happens in an instant so you have to be on the look out for it.

Pupil dilation

He can't control his pupils, therefore if they dilate it's a good indication that he finds you attractive or interesting. This method can be flawed – if you're in very dim or bright light, his pupils will dilate or contract to compensate.

Mirroring

Mirroring is the big body-language clue. It's when one person copies the other's movements or body positioning. If his posture or the positioning of his arms and legs mirrors yours, it's considered that he has an affinity with you. This happens naturally without any conscious effort when you like someone. You can test this by moving your posture and watching if he follows.

Body language clusters

It's a common myth that if someone folds their arms then they're defensive – but they may also be trying to enhance their cleavage or feeling a little chilly. To make sure you don't misinterpret a change in his mood, look for clusters of four changes in body language. If he turns in towards you when you're talking, leans in closer to talk, smiles more and is making more eye contact, he's definitely liking you more.

IS LOVE IN THE AIR?

TOP TIP

- Stick to the arm or hand region for appropriate touching.

Intentional touching

Touching is a powerful method of communication that can convey a number of messages, from empathy to attraction. Men can interpret touching by women as an availability for sex rather than a flirtation, so avoid being over familiar unless sex is your objective.

'Signs that he likes you' checklist

- Eyeline triangle
- Dilated pupils
- Mirroring body language
- Smiling more
- Good eye contact
- Leans in when he talks
- Mirrors my speech
- Mirrors my breathing
- Intentional touching
- Four changes in body language
- Preening himself.

Activity Spot the signs

- Using the checklist above as a guide, see how many of these apply during a conversation with friends. It's probably well over half. Get used to looking for the signs against a mental checklist.

- Use your mental checklist to see how your potential dates rate against it. If after a conversation you're getting less than half, review your position.

IS LOVE IN THE AIR?

How to tell if he doesn't fancy you

There will be times when, despite positive initial signs, he simply doesn't feel as strongly as you – with your intuition and super-honed skills you'll probably spot it, but if you're in doubt read on.

CASE STUDY

After one of my flirting classes, Paul was brave enough to approach a lady in a bar in full view of the rest of the group. The woman initially looked pleased – she turned to talk to him and was leaning in and smiling in animated conversation. We all gushed how well he was doing. Gradually she started to lean away, then her body turned away, she put her handbag on the bar in front of her as a barrier, her eye contact lessened and she stopped smiling. She started looking round the room for someone to rescue her. Eventually she jumped off her chair and left. Paul couldn't see where he had gone wrong, but we could. We could also see the lady on the next bar stool, who was trying to catch his eye. Once pointed in the right direction, he had a great evening.

Synchronisation

When you're getting on well, the conversation flows, each of you knows instinctively when to talk and when to listen. It's punctuated with little gestures, laughter and touching at appropriate moments. When you're out of synch the conversation feels awkward and doesn't flow – you may interrupt each other before the others finished, or talk over the top.

Barriers

When we want to keep a bit of space between ourselves and another person we put something between us. This can simply be crossing your arms or putting your ankle on your knee and keeping your shin between you, or it could be achieved with props, such as a folded coat or a menu. It tells the recipient, 'This is a line I don't want you to cross – keep back.'

TOP TIP

◆ Talk for about or less than 50% of the time, and don't let the other person have to make all the conversation.

Creating space

When we're getting intimate with someone, we lean in toward them to close the gap – conversely, if someone is getting too close we'll either do a little subconscious bob back or create more space by leaning away.

◉⚡ TOP TIP

♦ Once you've noticed four changes, mentally replay what was happening or being said at the point he started to change. Was it something you said or did? Address it and see if his body language starts improving.

'Signs that he doesn't fancy you' checklist

♦ Avoiding or lessening eye contact
♦ Trying to make eye contact with other people
♦ Conversation getting out of synch (awkward pauses, stilted)
♦ Several body language changes (rule of 4)
♦ They're not or stop smiling
♦ Hands covering face, chin resting on hand
♦ Staring onto their drink or space
♦ Creating space
♦ Putting barriers between you (arms, bags, menus, coats, etc).

Activity **Giving the signs**

● When you're with friends, act through the list above and see how quickly they get the message. Are some people more perceptive than others or are you getting more accomplished at it? Remember to explain what you were doing.

● Review your potential dates in your head. Did you notice any of them giving you more than four of these at one time? Did you carry on regardless or backtrack to the root of it? What are you going to do differently in future when you notice negative changes?

IS LOVE IN THE AIR?

Avoiding bad body language

Most bad body language is unintentional and easily corrected. Nevertheless, it is difficult to spot in ourselves.

1 Lack of eye contact

What it says I'm shifty, I lack confidence or I'm not interested.

How to correct it See Day 39.

2 Hands on hips (usually with legs apart)

What it says I'm a sexually aggressive female and I'm challenging you.

How to correct it Stand with your legs together, one foot in front of the other, to give you more height and a long curvy look. Hold something in your hand to stop you going for your hip.

3 Angling or leaning away

What it says I'm not interested in you, I want to create some space between us.

How to correct it If they've invaded your space, take a step back. Ensure when you're talking that you mirror their posture and positioning by turning in towards them and leaning in when you speak.

4 Propping your face up with your hand

What is says I'm so bored I can't be bothered to hold my head up.

How to correct it Sit on a chair with arms. Keep your head up and rest your chin on the back of your hand or fingers to look interested.

5 Collar fiddler

What it says You or this situation is making me uncomfortable, or I'm lying.

IS LOVE IN THE AIR?

How to correct it Be aware of what your hands are doing. If they do accidentally find themselves round your neck, slip them up to your hair and give it a sexy quick plump or preen.

6 Walking hunched over

What it says I'm trying not to draw attention to myself and I suffer from low self-esteem.

How to correct it Pull your stomach in and shoulders back, and thrust your chest out. This gives you an instant look of confidence.

7 Slouching in your seat

What it says I'm too cool to sit up and pay attention. If you want to get intimate with me you're going to have to do all the work.

How to correct it We're back to being naked again. If someone whipped all your kit off would you assume the same position? Sit up square – that way he'll be able to manoeuvre closer to you more easily.

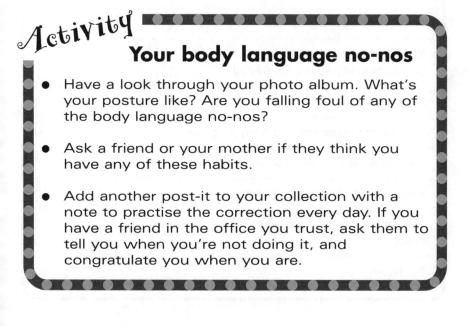

Activity
Your body language no-nos

- Have a look through your photo album. What's your posture like? Are you falling foul of any of the body language no-nos?

- Ask a friend or your mother if they think you have any of these habits.

- Add another post-it to your collection with a note to practise the correction every day. If you have a friend in the office you trust, ask them to tell you when you're not doing it, and congratulate you when you are.

IS LOVE IN THE AIR?

Pit stop 3 – how are you doing?

Congratulations, you're over half way through your programme. The combination of proactively looking for your man along with honing all the wonderful skills that will make you irresistible and able to pick up on all his gestures is starting to pay dividends. Prior to a full-scale assault on pulling at work, before swiftly moving on to dating etiquette and ultimately love and relationships, we're going to measure just how much you've achieved and plot where you should be channelling your efforts for maximum success in the remainder of the book.

As part of today's activity you will fill in the table below.

Score:
- 2 for strongly agree
- 1 for agree
- 0 for disagree

Area of observation	Score	Day 79
You are looking more confident.		
You are feeling more confident.		
You have, or you are on the way to completing your chosen objective from Day 30.		
You are people-watching more.		
You are more aware of your body language.		
You find it easier to make conversation.		
You are more confident with strangers.		
The people around you have noticed a change in you.		
TOTAL		

IS LOVE IN THE AIR?

Activity

Check your progress

Do this activity when you're feeling fresh and give top-of-mind responses for an accurate result.

- Flick back to Day 25 and complete the final column. Indicate its status (e.g. pulled/ongoing/finished) and mark out of 10 (1 being the lowest and 10 the highest) for how successful you feel it's been.

- How do you feel about your progress? If you've been following the book to the letter you should be getting some positive leads and feeling very pleased with yourself by now.

  If you're not satisfied with your progress, why? Are your expectations overly high? Have you not been completing the exercises? Are you lacking momentum? Don't worry, you've still got the second half of the programme to get you back on track. If you haven't subscribed for the text service that complements the book, why not start on Day 61 to keep your motivation high.

- Complete the first column of the table opposite and add up your total.

  If you scored:

  11–16 You're totally in the zone. If you're not already well into dating, success is just around the corner.
  6–10 Your motivation is on the right track. Supercharge it by reviewing the days related to the sections where you marked yourself 0 or 1.
  0–5 You could do with a bit of a friendly boost. Surround yourself with positive people and give anyone who saps your confidence and enthusiasm a wide berth until you feel your levels rising.

IS LOVE IN THE AIR?

Your notes

CHAPTER 9

BAGGING THE BEAU AT WORK

Launching the flirt at work

By now you're raring to go and your people radar is honed. Because of the high chance of success balanced with a potentially sensitive environment I've reserved this section until you're on top form. In this chapter we look at the pros and cons of pulling at work.

> **FACT:** The workplace is the area where the majority of people find their partners.

Romantic relationships at work are every HR Manager's nightmare. With a growing litigious culture in the UK, the last thing an employer wants is to be in a war zone following a break-up or, worse, a sexual harassment case. In the USA some companies require you to sign a love contract to indemnify them against any legal action as a result of your relationship. I was considering bringing in something similar at work, when my assistant announced she'd fallen madly in love with a guy in another department. It was swiftly abandoned.

Unlike all the other dating scenarios, you have to work in your office every day. You don't want to do anything that will jeopardise your relationships with others in the office, or your employment.

Pros	Cons
More choice if you work in a larger organisation.	Less opportunities in smaller organisations.
Can research potential dates with colleagues.	If it ends horribly you'll still have to face them.
Plenty of opportunities to mix with them.	Be careful that your advances aren't considered harassment.
You get to see them regularly when you're dating.	
It's free!	

Most sexual harassment cases are brought by women against men. The reason for this is partly that men are more likely to interpret 'friendly' gestures from women as meaning 'I'm sexually available'. When her friendliness is returned with unwanted sexual advances, you have the makings of a sexual harassment case. Most men will be flattered by your attention, but be aware of their rights if the feeling isn't mutual.

FACT: Sexual harassment is judged on how the recipient perceived it, not on how the other person intended it.

Activity

Work relationships

- Have a think back to any relationships you've had with people at work. How did they end? Well or badly?

- What would you do differently in future?

BAGGING THE BEAU AT WORK

How to pick the most likely dating targets

Today we're looking at prioritising the most likely candidates to approach.

1 Make a list of the people you find attractive.

2 Listen in on the office grapevine to see what you can find out about them. Single, just broken up, actively looking or taken? Lovely bloke, womaniser, bit of a git?

3 If you can, find out what their sports and interests are.

4 If you've got access to their electronic diary, check out their movements. If there are any projects or meetings you could get involved in, volunteer your services to the person responsible for it.

5 Find out how they get to work – drive, train, walk, cycle, etc. Do they do the same commute as you, or part of your commute?

6 Think back over your interactions with them. Was there any evidence of mutual attraction? Signs include positive eye contact / compliments / good positioning and synchronisation / body language (see Day 52).

TOP TIP

♦ Use the office grapevine to put it about that you're single and on the look out.

Activity

Who should you target?

Based on your research:

● Complete the table with the names of any likely candidates.

Name			
Attractiveness			
Personality			
Availability			
Daily contact			
Common ground			
Mutual attraction			
TOTAL			

● Under each name give a score in each area from 1 to 5, with 1 being the lowest and 5 the highest.

● Pick the man with the highest score as the most likely candidate.

BAGGING THE BEAU AT WORK

Finding the best gap to make your approach

You've got a wealth of information on this chap now – but if you suddenly appear at every meeting he has, whenever he goes for a coffee and on his route home, he's going to think you're a stalker. Instead, you need to use that information gradually, to make opportunities to develop a relationship with him. First, you need to find the best moments to approach him.

TOP TIP

♦ Keep your own council to keep your strategy from becoming the talking point of the office grapevine.

Activity
Focus on formations

● Get your people-spotting goggles on again. Watch the social interactions in the office and get used to spotting these formations. Even in large groups, the formations will always be broken down into these denominations. If you do a lot of networking this information is invaluable.

● Try breaking into the closed groups with an icebreaker (e.g. 'Does anyone know what the weather is forecast to be this weekend?') Compare the reaction you get to when you enter into the open formations. Do you find the closed groups harder and more hostile? Are the open groups more receptive?

● Now find an opportunity to approach your target man in an open formation with an icebreaker. How did you find it? How was he? And aren't you looking forward to chatting more with him!

There are clues as to the best time to approach someone. This information is fabulously useful in virtually every situation. It can be used in situations from nightclubs to business networking.

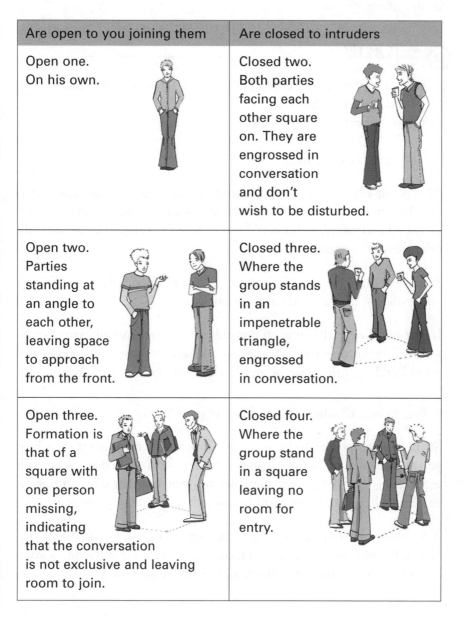

Are open to you joining them	Are closed to intruders
Open one. On his own.	Closed two. Both parties facing each other square on. They are engrossed in conversation and don't wish to be disturbed.
Open two. Parties standing at an angle to each other, leaving space to approach from the front.	Closed three. Where the group stands in an impenetrable triangle, engrossed in conversation.
Open three. Formation is that of a square with one person missing, indicating that the conversation is not exclusive and leaving room to join.	Closed four. Where the group stand in a square leaving no room for entry.

How to get your date at the office

You have three options when it comes to fixing a date with someone in the office.

◎⚹ TOP TIP

♦ Take your time – unless he's got another job, he's not going anywhere!

---

1 Get your mate to fix it

This is self-explanatory. It may smack of life in the playground but it can be more subtle – 'We're having some friends round at the weekend and wondered if you'd like to join us.' You appear as the only other singleton there.

If playground life suits the culture of your office, 'My mate fancies you, will you go out with her?' might work.

If you use, 'We're all going to the pub after work – would you like to join us?' make sure the friend who asks acts as host and gives you a good build up, otherwise he might think she fancies him/herself.

2 Get to him through his colleagues

Strike up a rapport with his mate, but make it obvious that it's not him you're attracted to but the other one. This is a tack that most men recognise – they'll egg their mate on, pointing out that you're attracted to him and that if he likes you he should do something about it.

If he hasn't picked up the signs, he may hang back until he's sure before he asks you. If he doesn't take the bait, use his friend as your confidant to get the inside track and broker a date for you.

CASE STUDY

Sally decided to get to Bruce via his colleague – unfortunately Sally wasn't too clear with her signals and Andrew thought he fancied her. Andrew asked her out and they've never looked back.

3 Ask him yourself

You know when the best opportunities are to approach him, you have a plethora of information on him to use for small talk, you've had loads of ice-breaking experience and you know which signs to look for. You're at work so you can build up a series of encounters until he asks you out or you're ready to ask him. Approach him when it's convenient and ask him if he'd like to go for a drink after work / coffee at lunchtime / mountain biking (or his preferred hobby) at the weekend.

⊙ TOP TIP

- Wear a distinctive scent that he will come to associate with you.

Activity **Make a work date**

- Choose your option from above – your choice will be influenced by the types of friends and colleagues you have, plus the culture of your organisation.

- How did you get on? Did you get your first choice man? If not, move on to man number 2. With the addition of the office jungle drums you never know who's going to be headed your way.

BAGGING THE BEAU AT WORK

Your notes

CHAPTER 10

MASTERING
DIFFICULT SITUATIONS

What's your confidence level?

Confidence is a game of two halves – take the confidence test and see if your halves balance.

1 When entering somewhere unfamiliar do you:
   a) March in and straight off to the loo/corner? ☐
   b) Enter with nervous anticipation? ☐
   c) Calmly pause to survey where you're planning to head to? ☐
2 Once in, do you:
   a) Hover expectantly? ☐
   b) Find somewhere quiet to sit? ☐
   c) Look for someone to approach? ☐
3 If you were to liken your confidence to a personality, who would it be?
   a) Emily Bishop ☐
   b) Madonna ☐
   c) Lorraine Kelly ☐
4 When someone compliments you on your dress, do you:
   a) Thank them? ☐
   b) Dismiss it? ☐
   c) Blush with embarrassment? ☐
5 If you get into a confrontation with a colleage, do you:
   a) Keep your cool and make your point? ☐
   b) Keep your trap shut, but beat yourself up for not saying something? ☐
   c) Go to pieces and completely lose it? ☐
6 How would a friend who observed the confrontation react?
   a) 'Take a chill pill Miss Hysterical.' ☐
   b) 'That was uber cool, go girl!' ☐
   c) 'Wasn't there a point you wanted to make?' ☐

Score

	a)	b)	c)		a)	b)	c)
1	2	1	3	**4**	3	2	1
2	2	1	3	**5**	3	2	1
3	1	3	2	**6**	1	3	2

Activity

How confident are you?

- Add up your combined score.

- Add up your 'internal' and 'perceived' scores.

  Internal Q1 + Q3 + Q5 = _____

  Perceived Q2 + Q4 + Q6 = _____

If your combined score is:

14–18 You have good levels of internal and perceived confidence. You can cope with most situations that life throws at you and if you can't, you do a good job of looking like you can.

10–13 Are your internal and perceived levels equal?

If so, work a little on both – each will increase the other as it rises.

If not, work on your perceived confidence – as people start to react to your confident exterior your internal confidence will get a boost and start to grow itself.

6–9 Have you filled this in when you were feeling off-form? Try it again when you're feeling more optimistic. If your score doesn't improve, you owe it to yourself to start 'thinking confident'. You'll really benefit from faking your perceived confidence until your internal confidence rises. Read all about it in tomorrow's lesson.

MASTERING DIFFICULT SITUATIONS

Are you keeping up? Do you need some help? If you've not already subscribed, why not try the daily text messaging service for extra encouragement and support. Just text 'Settled 61' to 80881 now.

Each set of messages costs £1.50. Please see page x for full terms and conditions.

How to ooze confidence

Imagine confidence as an egg. Your **perceived** or outward confidence (the bit that everyone can see and takes in) is the shell. Your **internal** confidence is the inside. It's impossible for anyone to tell from the shell whether you're hard-boiled, soft or even off!

My corporate work involves teaching employees how to boost their perceived confidence. In an ideal world, employers would love employees to be brimming with internal confidence – however, their limited time as well as budgets don't permit. Besides, their clients only see the perceived confidence, so what better place to start. For great results and well-being, confidence is something to practise in every environment, from work to dating.

You could spend years learning to 'love yourself' and letting your energy be a beautiful white shining light which beams out over mankind – but you could be hit by a bus tomorrow. There's another way which gives great **perceived** results. By acting confident, people respond to you as if you are confident, which makes you feel confident, so you act more confident … people respond to you as if you are more confident … which makes you feel more confident … and before you know it you're feeling and looking confident.

Boost your perceived confidence

1 Look confident – get your body language and posture right. See Day 54.
2 Sound confident – get your tonality right and say everything with conviction. See Day 15.
3 Use confident language – don't draw attention to your flaws, don't put yourself down at the end of sentences.

Boost your internal confidence

1 Stop reinforcing negative beliefs. **Think positive**. Say to yourself, 'They'll be interested in me because I'm interesting.'
2 Stop telling yourself that you're not confident. **Act confident** until you are eventually being confident naturally.
3 **Talk about feeling good** – people love positivity. If you're feeling good, happy, excited, enthusiastic, then say so.
4 Avoid 'musterbation'. Instead of saying 'I must' or 'I should', **reverse those thoughts** to 'I can' or 'I will' or 'I'll risk it'.
5 **Take risks** and don't take rejection personally – there's an ocean of opportunities out there.

TOP TIP

♦ E-mail me for a fact sheet on boosting confidence. See the Introduction for my address.

Activity **Boost your confidence**

● Depending on what your scores were yesterday, focus on one or other of the points above. Even if your scores were good, try souping up your perceived confidence and pay attention to the reactions of the people around you.

● If somebody asks you a question you're not sure about, give them the answer as if you're positive and watch them believe your confidence. (Obviously if it's a life and death situation please tell them afterwards that you're not 100% sure!)

● How impressed are you by the reactions to your boosted perceived confidence? Is your inner confidence gaining ground?

● You should still be saying the contents of your post-it notes daily – say it loud and with conviction.

MASTERING DIFFICULT SITUATIONS

How to deal with difficult people

Not many people enjoy dealing with difficult people, although being the eldest of three girls I love a challenge myself. We can't help who we fall for and nobody's perfect, so if your chap is a little bit challenging, nip it in the bud

> **FACT:** Women often suffer from the 'need to please' and end up agreeing to things they would rather not.

before he expects to get his own way all the time. Most of us get into the habit at an early age of dealing with our conflicts in the same way. It can be a very tough habit to break.

CASE STUDY

Jo consistently gave in to Steve's requests against her wishes. He had a way of talking through every reason she could give him until she ran out of excuses not to. The first time she used the broken record technique on him she found herself out of her comfort zone. However, when she held her ground Steve relented. It took a couple more times until she was comfortable with the technique, but she's never looked back since and uses it regularly with everyone, from family to work.

If you're being harassed to do something you don't want to do, use a broken record technique, whereby you do not enter into a negotiation or an explanation to their request, you simply repeat the same phrase to all their questions.

'Do you want to go out next Friday?'
'I'm sorry, it's not convenient for me.'
'What are you doing then?'
'I'm sorry, it's not convenient for me.'
'Can't you change your plans?'
'I'm sorry, it's not convenient for me.'
'Surely you'd rather be going out with me?'
'I'm sorry, it's not convenient for me.'

This marvellous phrase can be replaced with just about anything.

'I'm not planning to do that.'
'I'm strapped for cash right now.'
'I'm sorry, I have other plans.'

Broken record statements should be:

◆ Brief
◆ Short on detail
◆ Delivered without change.

When they realise that this is the only answer they're going to get, people (including children) soon get the message and stop asking.

Activity

Use the broken record technique

● Identify people whom you feel manipulate you into doing things you would rather not do. When you're around them, have your broken record technique on standby. If they do corner you, do not enter into a debate or justify your broken record statement, just keep saying it until they stop asking.

● How did that feel? Difficult, easier than you expected, nerve-racking but brilliant now it's over? How did they react? Were they puzzled, did they acquiesce, were they angered? If they were angered, this person wrongly thinks they have some control over you and you need to put your foot down with them or give them a wide berth.

● If you feel your date pushing you against your decision, use the broken record technique on him to make sure you maintain an equal powerbase in the relationships.

MASTERING DIFFICULT SITUATIONS

What do you bring to difficult situations?

Very few people are difficult all on their own. What is your behaviour contributing to the situation?

CASE STUDY

Kate and Laurie got to the stage where they could barely talk to each other without raising their voices, as each wanted to get the first dig in and have the last word. With a bit of transactional analysis they revised their behaviour and now either avoid petty arguments or have a civilised debate.

Transactional analysis is a very simple way of looking at how your behaviour is affecting a situation. If you study your behaviour you'll probably find that you don't behave the same way in every situation. Everyone knows somebody who instantly puts them on the attack or defensive; likewise there are others who get off lighter than you would normally treat people.

Kate	Laurie
Parent	Parent
Adult	Adult
Child	**Child**

You can see in the case of Kate and Laurie that they were both initially responding to each other as children.

CASE STUDY

My other half had his car vandalised – unbeknown to him the insurance had run out the day before. He had an important meeting to go to and we were going on holiday in a couple of days. He was overwhelmed with the situation and I took over before giving him a chance to get his thoughts. Things went from bad to worse – eventually Glyn had a fit and blamed me for everything (which clearly wasn't my fault). I took a step back from the situation and let him get on with it himself. He got it resolved, it saved me a lot of hassle and we were all happy.

Elizabeth	Glyn
Parent	Parent
Adult	Adult
Child	**Child**

Initially I took on the role of parent trying to fix things. Glyn reverted to child to such an extent that he eventually had a huff.

Elizabeth	Glyn
Parent	Parent
Adult	**Adult**
Child	Child

Glyn got his act together and sorted it out. I could have reacted as a parent and insisted I deal with it, or as a child and had hysterics because he accused me of messing it up. However, it was more appropriate to act like an adult and let him get on with it himself.

Activity

Interact as adults

- Look at your more challenging relationships. Which role do you tend to take? And which role does the other party take? What could you do differently to put the relationship back on an adult footing?

- If you have narrowed your dates down to one special man, which role are you taking in the relationship? Are you both adults? Are you playing the parent to his child or vice versa? Or do you both behave like children? For the relationship to be stable and both parties to feel equal, you should be aiming for an adult–adult match.

MASTERING DIFFICULT SITUATIONS

Your notes

CHAPTER 11

DATING RULES

Dating etiquette – the rules

Gone are the days when ladies were ladies and men were gentlemen. Men are totally confused when it comes to what they should and shouldn't do – the traditional male bastions have disappeared as the boundaries of male/female roles in courtship have blurred over the years.

CASE STUDY

Bev had her first date with Simon. They had met over the internet and had enjoyed chatting online and on the phone. Simon admired how ballsy and independent Bev had been during their conversations. When the bill came he asked her if she wanted to go halves. Bev was mortified – her vision of a knight in shining armour didn't include a request to go Dutch. She became frosty towards him with disappointment. He thought she didn't fancy him. When he e-mailed her to ask what had gone wrong, she said that whilst actually she has no objection to paying her way, she thought it was the place of a gentleman to pay on the first date and a bit tight of him to expect her to pay half. He explained that her fiercely independent stance had led him to believe that it would offend her if he had just paid. They had a re-run of the first date, Simon treated her like a princess and everyone was happy.

The government is determined that we're all going to work till we drop. You're not even allowed to have babies and enjoy being at home in their formative years – you're expected to drop it and be back in the office virtually the following afternoon! However, most blokes still expect you to be a woman at home, e.g. washing, cooking and cleaning, but in the vein of true equality he'll let you take the bins out too (apologies to any men out there who truly do their half, you are in the minority). When it comes to forming a relationship, all our basic instincts kick in. Men are designed to procreate and women to nurture. You've got something that he wants. If you give it to him readily and immediately, it can have less value and the relationship is in decline before it's run through the three stages of Lust, Love and Attachment (more of this on Day 77). Seduction is heady and not something to be rushed. Regardless of how you've got together – whether you've approached him, he's approached you, you've met online, in the office, or on the bus – you'll follow the same rules from here.

The rules

1 Dating safely
2 Preparing for the date
3 Dressing for success
4 Conversation objectives
5 Building the sexual tension
6 Ending the date
7 Getting the second date
8 Life after the first date
9 Test if he's for you
10 What if he doesn't …

◎✦ TOP TIP

♦ Following the rules is like following a diet – it's only effective if you stick to it.

Activity Make the rules work for you

● Consider your dating patterns to date. Do you have your own rules that have worked for you? Are there any particular areas where you feel your dating ritual starts to unravel? Can you match that point into the rule topics above?

DATING RULES

Rule 1 – Dating safely

Gone are the days when people lived in communities and everyone had some connection, however spurious, to your date. Without that vital term of reference, follow the tips to make sure you play safe and stay safe.

> **FACT:** It's highly unlikely that anything awful (apart from not hitting it off) will happen to you on a first date.

♦ **Be careful accepting drinks from strangers**

Say 'No' unless you can see your drink being poured and never leave your glass unattended.

♦ **Don't drink too much on a first date**

If you don't know him, you need to have your wits about you.

♦ **Initially arrange to meet for coffee or lunch rather than dinner**

If you don't fancy him, just say, 'You're a great person, but unfortunately, not what I was looking for.'

♦ **Stick to an area that's well lit with lots of people around**

Don't arrange to meet in car parks or quiet rural pubs.

♦ **Don't give out personal details**

Have a mobile number you use for dating – only give him your other numbers when you know him a bit better and you feel confident that it's going to last more than a couple of dates.

DATING RULES

◆ **Trust your gut instinct**

If something doesn't feel right, make your excuses and leave. Make sure a friend knows you've left and call them when you're home safely.

◆ **Listen to his relationship history**

Reading between the lines may give you clues, e.g. if every girl-friend dumps him after the first date, or he hates every woman he's ever dated, there is a problem.

◆ **Give the details of your meeting to several friends**

Get them to phone you an hour into the date to check you're OK, then you phone them a few hours later to report in again.

◆ **Don't invite strangers to your home**

Equally, don't go to theirs until you know them very well.

Activity

Stay safe

◆ Learn the above tips and make sure you always follow them.

Rule 2 – Preparing for your date

When I was in my teens my grandmother had very straightforward rules about a first date. If a chap wanted to take you out, he had to collect you from home, at the allocated time, and drop you back safely afterwards. Meeting the relatives was enough of a deterrent to ensure nothing untoward happened. Gone are the days when you would invite a stranger to your house for a first date.

CASE STUDY

My grandmother was doing her usual spying bit one night when my new chap came to pick me up. He was very polite and graciously answered her interrogation. When I returned later she commented that he seemed a very nice man, pity that he drove a nasty little white van. I pointed out that his nasty little white van was actually a Porche.

If you haven't got a concerned relative calling the shots, abide by the following:

◆ Plan to be on time. Good manners and civility cost nothing. If you play by the 'treat 'em mean keep 'em keen' rules, don't be surprised if you get a taste of your own medicine.

◆ If you're going to be more than 10–15 minutes late, call. A lady's prerogative to be late doesn't extend indefinitely.

⌖ TOP TIP

◆ If it's a blind date paint him an alluring picture of who to look for.

DATING RULES

◆ Keep contact before the date to a minimum. Don't spend hours on the phone – it'll spoil your allure.

◆ Let him choose the venue – it'll speak volumes about his taste and how much he rates you as a date. Remember to tell him if you have any food preferences or allergies.

◆ If he asks you to choose, don't just pick the most expensive place in town. Go for somewhere with a bit of class.

◆ Arrange with your 'call girl' to call you 30 minutes into the date.

◆ Get yourself in a calm state of mind – you don't want to appear too enthusiastic.

TOP TIP

◆ To ground your nerves, sit with both feet on the floor and concentrate on your breathing. Breathe in for 3 and out for 4. Focus on the counting and on breathing out for longer than you breath in. Repeat until you can feel your pulse settle and your breathing calm.

Activity
Be prepared

● Fail to plan and you're planning to fail. Ensure you have checked off the entire list opposite before going on your first date.

● Learn to get control of your nerves. Practise the exercise above whenever you feel the need arising.

DATING RULES

Rule 3 – Dressing for success

⊙ ↗ TOP TIP

◆ Men are generally willing to spend that little bit extra doing something special for a date, make sure you're dressed for the occasion.

Your wardrobe should be packed full of options following your makeover on Day 7. The dating etiquette rules for dressing are as follows.

◆ Dress for the man that you want, not what you've had in the past.

◆ Play to their physiological tendencies and go for colour and shape, but avoid looking tarty (too tight or too short or too cut away).

◆ Let your outfit leave something to the imagination. Wear layers so you can peel away the clothes later to reveal a tantalising glimpse of flesh later in the date.

◆ Exfoliate and moisturise all visible flesh and use a light-reflecting lotion. Your skin will be visibly radiant when the light hits it and you'll have a healthy glow.

◆ Remove all superfluous hair. British men tend to dislike it.

◆ Dab a finger of your vaginal secretions (not menstrual) behind ears and wrists for a devastating natural pheromone perfume.

◆ Spray your body with perfume – as you get warmer it will mingle with your natural aromas.

◆ Don't apply fake tan the day of your date – it leaves a pungent aroma that will interfere with the effect of your natural pheromones.

◆ Use a teeth-whitening treatment the week before.

- Avoid alcohol for 48 hours before the date and take milk thistle to cleanse the liver and brighten the skin and eyes.
- Wear hear in a style that won't collapse if you touch it – men aren't attracted to rigid hair anyway.
- Wear a necklace or bracelet to touch and tease with later in the date.

TOP TIP

- Wear a lip plump – it mimics the lips' natural fullness signal of sexual arousal. Top it off with gloss so his eyes are drawn to your mouth.

Your look has to do two things:

1 Appeal to his sexual desires without sending the impression that you're a dead cert.
2 The glowing skin, teeth and eyes will appeal to him on a more basic survival of the fittest level, i.e. this woman is good breeding stock.

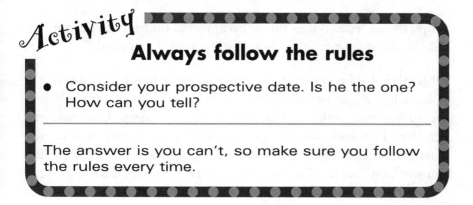

Activity

Always follow the rules

- Consider your prospective date. Is he the one? How can you tell?

The answer is you can't, so make sure you follow the rules every time.

Rule 4 – Conversation objectives

You know how to make conversation and what to say, but in order to assess the suitability of a date, and for the dating rules to work, you must include objectives. This links back to Chapter 1 where we looked at whether you kept habitually going for the same type of man or choosing men whose values don't match yours.

It was a standing joke in our family that when a new boy's name was mentioned mum wanted to know: Who is he? Where does he come from? What does he do? What do his parents do?

All were considered vital points before determining his suitability, regardless of whether you liked him or not. I was horrified the other day to find myself giving my ten-year-old son a similar grilling on a girl I'd seen him with!

Objective 1 Make him feel comfortable, let him know you're interested in him.

Objective 2 Use small talk to develop rapport. Avoid discussing your ex, work dilemmas and anything negative. Keep it positive.

Objective 3 Find out as much background on him as you can: 'So, tell me about your family / job / changes on the horizon?'

Objective 4 Use personal disclosure to make him feel comfortable. If he tells you something personal, return the trust and tell him something too, being careful not to go too deep into anything negative. If there's something that you value bring it into the conversation and observe his response, e.g. 'I can see myself travelling and working abroad. Have you ever worked abroad?' If he says, 'No, I religiously go to my mum's every Sunday for lunch,' there aren't a lot of shared values there.

Objective 5 Look for clues in his previous relationships as to what makes him tick and what to avoid in your developing relationship. If he hated the fact that his last girlfriend never shaved her legs, or spent

DATING RULES

too much time on the phone to her mother, avoid doing the same. Avoid too much personal disclosure yourself on negative aspects of previous relationships. Men don't like to discuss your dating history as they would prefer to be your first.

If it gets too heavy or boring move the conversation on: 'Listen to us. We're on our first date and we're bringing our baggage with us – tell me about the next holiday you have planned.'

TOP TIP

+ Don't drink too much.
+ Don't talk about sex, or make references to sex.
+ Don't swear, belch or fart.
+ Don't take phone calls (apart from your safety check).
+ Don't be rude or negative to the waiting staff.
+ If he thinks you're a lady he's more likely to treat you as one.

Activity

Plan your conversation

● Make a list of your values and things that are important to you.

● Plan ways to slip them into the conversation.

● Observe his body language as well as the words when he answers you. Is it congruent with what he's saying?

● Keep a mental note of his compatibility in terms of what you want.

DATING RULES

Rule 5 – Building the sexual tension

Only if you fancy him and you're satisfied with the responses to your conversation objectives should you indulge his senses from a discrete distance.

> **FACT:** Playing with hair when you fancy someone releases pheromones, the sex hormone.

A feast for his eyes

Using plenty of eye contact and smiling, get a little more playful with the objects around you. Bring his gaze to your face, neck and wrists by choosing to touch them subtly in turn.

- Gently play with your necklace to draw attention to your décolleté.
- With your elbows on the table and your wrists up by your face, gently and slowly stroke the inside of your wrist. Or playfully run your finger through your bracelet.
- Draw attention to the face and neck by playing with your hair. Sweep it away from your face or pile it on your head and let it fall.
- Draw attention to your mouth by touching your lips, either covertly with a napkin or overtly with your fingers.

TOP TIP

- Men are inclined to read friendly signals as signs of sexual availability, so don't be overly friendly with him until you decide you definitely fancy him.
- Do not be overtly sexual. Gripping the stem of your wine glass and running your fingers up and down it will lead him to believe it's in the bag.

DATING RULES

Where appropriate give him a gentle touch or squeeze on the arm or hand for a lasting positive effect.

Remove that extra layer of clothing you put on earlier to give him that little extra flash of flesh.

Close the gap by leaning in when you talk. Use your tonality by lowering the pitch and volume of your voice so he leans closer to listen for an intimate conversation.

TOP TIP

♦ Don't overstay your first date. Leave when he's enjoying you most, to make him want more.

Activity
Send him signals

● We were all programmed to do these things naturally so don't give too much thought to deliberately doing them. Once you're in the zone it will happen as a matter of course. However, a little 'hair plump' and a 'reveal' won't hurt to help get things moving.

● Observe how he responds to your playful flirt. Do you notice any body language changes in him?

● How do you feel when you're being at your most flirtatious? Fabulous, sexy, naughty, ridiculous? You're doing what comes naturally and giving off all the signs Mother Nature programmed him to look for, so enjoy it and watch your skills grow.

DATING RULES

Rule 6 – Ending the date

Make sure you get the second date by ending this one before it's reached it's natural conclusion. Do you think Price Charming would have been quite so pursuant of Cinderella if she'd stayed till the bitter end, got lashed with the Ugly sisters and ravished him in the courtyard? If you're having a fabulous time and you don't want it to end, leave him with that feeling too. He'll be all the more keen to arrange date number two.

CASE STUDY

I shared a house with some guys who had a three date rule. If she was a seven-star plus woman, they were okay about paying for everything for three dates, but if no significant 'progress' had been made she was packed off in line with the rule. Men don't expect too much on a first date (that's not to say they wouldn't like it). If a guy does expect more than a thank you on a first date, don't waste your time on him.

TOP TIP

♦ Take a cab home, it avoids any long kissing in the car park or attempts to pop up for coffee. Leave them wanting more.

Closing the date

Use an early appointment as the excuse to close the date: 'I really hate to put an end to the conversation, but I've got an early start in the morning and I'd better be heading off. Would you mind asking the waiter to call me a cab?'

If he offers you a lift, decline graciously: 'That's very kind of you, but no thank you. I've got to call my girlfriend on the way home for a de-brief and I can't do that with you there.'

Paying the bill

As a rule of thumb, the person who did the inviting should pick up the bill.

DATING RULES

- If he offers to pay, let him.
- Don't offer to go Dutch if you're not paying.
- If he asks if you want to go Dutch, unless he's an impoverished sex god, make a mental note never to see him again.

The goodbye

When your cab arrives, thank him using very positive language: 'I've had a lovely time, you've been great company and the food was delicious – thank you.'

Make the invitation for him to call: 'We must do it again some time – why don't you give me a call when you're free? I'm busy for the next few days but Thursday afternoon would be a good time to ring.'

Confuse his senses by giving him good body contact, but only a brief peck on the cheek. Do not engage in a long snogging session – it spoils the 'leaving him wanting more' ending.

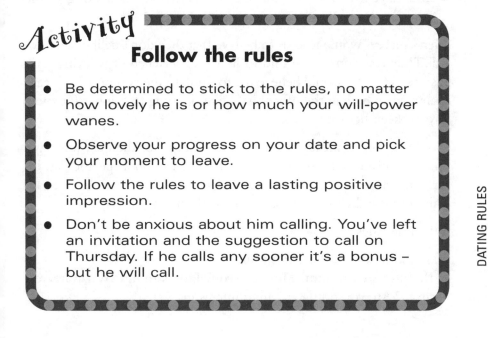

Activity
Follow the rules

- Be determined to stick to the rules, no matter how lovely he is or how much your will-power wanes.

- Observe your progress on your date and pick your moment to leave.

- Follow the rules to leave a lasting positive impression.

- Don't be anxious about him calling. You've left an invitation and the suggestion to call on Thursday. If he calls any sooner it's a bonus – but he will call.

DATING RULES

Are you keeping up? Do you need some help? If you've not already subscribed, why not try the daily text messaging service for extra encouragement and support. Just text 'Settled 71' to 80881 now.

Each set of messages costs £1.50. Please see page x for full terms and conditions.

Rule 7 – Getting the second date

If you're going to make contact with him, the **only** time you can do it is by text immediately after the date. It's good manners to say thank you, so if you feel you didn't do a good enough job of it in person send a short text. If this starts a game of tennis texts, don't send more than three back – use your last text to say goodnight and you're looking forward to speaking to him in the week.

If you leave it till the following morning it'll look like you're courting him. Men are the hunter gatherers – leave him to do the chasing.

Do not be tempted to call him just because your mind is telling you the following:

◆ Your answer machine may not have recorded his message.
◆ You can't trust mobiles and maybe his message is floating in the ether somewhere.

Men's surveys would lead us to believe that they don't deliberately not call. They just don't get round to it. My experience of working with many single men would believe me to think to the contrary. I've heard many a man brag in the office that he's not going to call her for a few days to keep her on her toes.

However, you've already said that you are 'busy for the next few days' and have planted the suggestion for him to call on a specific day. It's far enough away for it still to fit in with his 'treat 'em mean' philosophy and he'll have made a mental note of the day.

When he rings:

◆ Sound pleased to hear from him.
◆ Be interested in him. 'How are you? How's things? What are you up to? Are you doing anything interesting?' etc.

DATING RULES

- If he's rung on the suggested day, when he asks for a date, ask what day suits him – only volunteer your availability if it's minimal. If he says Tuesday, you say Wednesday would be better for you. Telling him you're free from now till Christmas is not a good idea.

If he doesn't ring on the day, don't despair. If the signs were as good as you thought and you made a convincing job of letting him know you liked him, he'll call. When he does call:

- Don't be stroppy.
- Don't agree to date the forthcoming weekend.
- Only agree to the following week or weekend after.

TOP TIP

- Arrange your second date on a weekday and take a cab.

Activity
Don't call him!

- Follow this rule to the letter. If you can't be trusted not to call him, give his number to a mate and destroy every copy you have of it.

- How did it feel not calling him? Was it as awful waiting for the phone to ring when you knew you had the pre-suggested date to wait for? If you're double-dating, how much easier was it with the second guy you tried it on? Are you feeling more in control of your destiny?

DATING RULES

Rule 8 – Life after the first date

You'll have arranged your second date for a weeknight. Follow the same rules as before.

1 End the date in full swing. Apologise for having to dash again, but promise next time you'll have to do it on a weekend and really make a night of it.

2 Ask for a cab home.

3 Let him pay.

4 Thank him and tell him how much you've enjoyed his company.

5 Instead of a peck, give him a proper kiss, but don't let it develop into a full-scale snog.

6 Pull back before it gets too intense. Stay in his intimate zone (12–18"), look him straight in the eye and tell him that you can't wait to do that again properly, but you've got to leave.

7 Let him know which is the best date and time to catch you. Don't give him more than one.

8 Text him immediately to thank him for the date and say how much you're looking forward to picking up where you left off.

TOP TIP

If he calls between dates to chat:

- ◆ Don't always be available to take all his calls.
- ◆ Don't spend too long on the phone.
- ◆ Always leave him with the impression you're glad he called.
- ◆ Only call him to return his calls or confirm arrangements.

When he calls to arrange the third date (and he will – you've now become a challenge, he's the hunter and you're about to be gathered!) if he calls on or before the suggested date, arrange a date for the next weekend. If he calls after the date, don't see him until the following week.

By the third date you've spent several hours with him – you know if this guy is making you tick or not. If the passion is building proceed with a good old-fashioned snog.

TOP TIP

♦ Absolutely **no** sex before the fourth date. You'll both be crazy with desire by the time you hit the bedroom (see Day 78 for the reasons why).

Reeling him in

● Promise yourself to stick to the rules.

● Get to know him, build the passion and enjoy the ensuing seduction.

● Don't be swayed by your friends to call him or to break the rules.

● Ask yourself how you feel when you're around him. How do you feel about yourself? About him? About you as a couple?

DATING RULES

Rule 9 – Test if he's for you

There are very good reasons why you don't jump into bed with him on the first three dates. You are:

◆ Getting to know him better
◆ Building a sexual crescendo
◆ Evaluating him as a potential Mr Right
◆ Playing to his basic instincts.

> **FACT:** Our hormones conspire against us when it comes to love and lust – don't let them cloud your judgement.

Depending on where you've met him (e.g. at work or at a recreational activity), you don't want to get a reputation. You may want to go on to date other people there and it's preferable to have a reputation for being hard, rather than easy, to get. Even in these days of equality it's still not socially acceptable for women to be overtly promiscuous. Men are keen to date sexually available women, but not necessarily keen to marry them, preferring the girl next door type as more stable stock.

Before you hit the sack answer the following questions.

1	Is he clear of all of my bad old dating habits?	Yes/No
2	Is he a 'type' that's likely to be compatible with me?	Yes/No
3	Does he respect me enough to take things at my pace?	Yes/No
4	Does he make me feel good about myself?	Yes/No
5	Do I feel good around him?	Yes/No
6	Is each date getting better?	Yes/No
7	Am I finding out more about him each date?	Yes/No
8	Does his dating history make sense?	Yes/No
9	Are his responses honest and congruent with what he's told me previously?	Yes/No
10	Does he have similar values to me?	Yes/No
11	Would I introduce this bloke to my mates?	Yes/No
12	Would I take him home to meet the parents?	Yes/No

DATING RULES

Activity

Is he right for you?

Answer the questions opposite.

If you've answered 'No' to:

1 Beware that you could be setting yourself up for a familiar cycle of disappointment. Proceed with caution.
2 Opposites attract, so this is OK if you've answered 'Yes' to most of the other questions.
3 It's nice to know he's keen but if he's uncomfortably forceful, what else will he try and bully you into?
4 If he doesn't make you feel good about yourself now, he never will – dump him for the sake of your self-esteem.
5 Is it because you're racked with nerves, or are you holding back to see if he's the one?
6 If you're not enjoying seeing him more at this stage, it doesn't bode well – are you seeing him just because you don't have a Plan B?
7 Are you in lust with an ideal? Is he slow to disclose information about himself, or has he got something to hide?
8 Probe like mad. What has he got to hide?
9 Women have a better gut reaction than men – trust it. What good reason could he have not to be honest with you? Is he trying too hard to make a favourable impression or has he got something to hide? Tread carefully.
10 Are they vastly dissimilar to yours – is he carnivore to your veggie? Can you live with it or will it eventually cause a problem when the infatuation wears off?
11 The mates test is a toughie. They can be highly critical, usually because they have your best interest at heart. Or is it your friends that are the problem? Are you constantly aware of their negative criticism? Perhaps you should think about a change of friends instead.
12 Is he not good enough for them? Is that because they think nobody will be good enough for you? Or, in your heart of hearts, do you know he's a wrong'un? If it's the latter, dump him while you can.

If you can answer yes to all of these questions then get ready to start a relationship with massive potential!

DATING RULES

Rule 10 – What if he doesn't ...

After date three, provided he's made it through the 'Is he right for me?' list, you're free to take things at your own pace. He's already gained a healthy respect for you and, although keen to get you in a compromising clinch, he'll follow your pace if he's the one.

What if he doesn't...

Q. Turn up on time for a date?
A. If he hasn't called to explain, give him 10–15 minutes then leave. A game on your phone is a distracting way to spend the time. Wait for him to call to apologise. If he doesn't, move onto your next prospect.

Q. Call me?
A. If he's right for you, he'll call. Don't be tempted to do the running, you'll only make a nuisance of yourself. Maybe he's not dating seriously and is seeing more than one person at a time. If he has an excuse every time he calls, for not calling, dump him – he has no class or manners.

Q. Like my friends?
A. Is it imperative you all get along? Is he seeing a different side of you around your friends that he doesn't recognise? Is he trying to isolate you from your friends to keep you to himself?

Q. Let me near his house or friends?
A. Is this guy who he says he is? Is he married? Has he inflated his circumstances to impress you? Be wary until you can find out more. If you can't clarify the situation, dump him and move on.

Q. Want to use a condom?
A. What fool has sex these days without a condom? Someone who doesn't care about themselves or you. The STD clinics cannot cope with the rocketing rates of infection. One of the highest growth groups is women over 45 years old. If you value your health and fertility – no condom, no sex.

Q. See me as often as I'd like?
A. How often do you want to see him? Is it reasonable to expect to see someone more than once or twice a week in the initial stages?

DATING RULES

Enquire discretely about his other commitments – he's got a life of his own, so don't expect him to give up his routine immediately. If he won't see you more than once or twice a month without a very good reason, dump him and move on.

Q. Want to terminate contact with his ex?
A. Is she the mother of his child? Did the relationship end amicably years ago? If so then it's permissible they have contact.

If she is clinging to a hope that something will rekindle and he is not discouraging her from that thought? In this case, he's either a coward, enjoys the attention or has no respect for you or her – in which case dump him and move on.

Q. Leave his wife?
A. What are you doing going out with a married man? Married men are no good, I can verify this from personal experience. If they're serious about forming a new relationship they'll make the effort to leave. Don't be suckered by stories that his wife doesn't understand him, or she's not been the same since she had the kids. If he promises to leave his wife (don't let him move in with you, rebound relationships don't last) and is still there three months later, dump him and move on, he's going to be nothing but trouble.

Activity
Solve your dilemma

- Pick your dating dilemma and consider the answer carefully. Have the courage to put a stop to any behaviour that will be detrimental to a mutually respectful relationship. Don't put up with it just because there's nothing better on the horizon. Invest your energy in finding someone else – don't waste it on this guy's bad behaviour.

DATING RULES

What women want in a long-term boyfriend

On a superficial level men tend to lust whatever is attractive that's dangled infront of their nose. Their teenage angst is about losing their virginity as quickly as a nasty spot on their chin, whereas girls fantasise about sharing it with the right person. We tend to take this with us into adulthood. You just need to look at the amount of women who swoon over the likes of Brad Pitt, George Clooney and even Will Young who is openly gay! You must differentiate between what is fantasty boyfriend material and what is long-term liveable with, to give you a wider choice of dates and your relationships the best chance of long-term success.

Don't send your man hunt off on a tangent by holding out for the fantasy relationship. I've come across idols who have been to die for on screen but are just as flawed as the next men (and not half as attractive without the lighting and flattering camera angles). Take our truth test to see if there is anything that's getting between you and a long-term relationship.

What women want

To be cared for
Not in a patronising or old fashioned way, even the most independent woman needs care and support in her relationships. Him being able to identify those times is critical.

To be respected
We need to feel valued.

Honesty
Trust is the glue that holds relationships together.

To be listened to
Communication is the bedrock of all good relationships. Women want to be able to have a conversation where he will listen and respond without him resorting to the 'nagging' tag.

Shared experiences
Great memories are the foundation of a good relationship, being able to share the good times and the bad times makes a relationship deep.

Room to grow

Men can fall into a long-term relationship rut, giving you the space and support to try out new things from jobs to sexual positions is vital to the long-term success of your relationship.

Pampering

Thoughtful surprises are lovely and show that you're still high on his agenda.

Activity

Telling fantasy dates from real ones

Answer the following questions:

1.	Ideally I'd like my boyfriend to be like Brad Pitt/Colin Firth.	True/False
2.	A guy has to match my preconceived standards for looks.	True/False
3	I prefer to date men with perfect manners.	True/False
4.	I like a man to be dressed stylishly for every occasion.	True/False
5.	Ideally he's got to be funny/charming and a bit dangerous.	True/False
6.	I'd like him to have money and status.	True/False
7.	He has to be popular with my friends and his.	True/False
8.	I find it attractive when a man is good at everything he tries.	True/False

Score yourself on the questions above. How many Trues did you score?

6–8 Your in love with the idea of a fantasy relationship and are destined for disappointment with 99% of the male population. Real long-term relationships have warts and all. You'll have to be prepared to lower some of your ideals and direct your focus on the points above to give a guy the chance to get close enough to win you over with a real relationship.

3–5 Which questions did you answer true to, are they a realistic combination? Of the friends you know in successful long-term relationships do their men have these attributes? Which ones could you consider swapping in the points above to increase your chance of developing a long-term relationship.

0–2 Well done, you have the best chance of growing a successful, long-term relationship. Focus on the points above to spot the plus points in a long-term relationship.

DATING RULES

What men want in a long-term girlfriend

My friend's mother used to say to her, 'to please a man is easy; they want a maid, a cook and a lover', to which she replied, 'fine, I'll hire the other two but look after the bedroom side myself.' With this fact in mind, it's easier to give men what they want, then grow into your relationship

> **FACT:** Once someone has formed a first impression it takes up to 21 further exposures in order for them to revise their opinion.

when you've got past the first few dates. Some may decry this as manipulative. However, if, like me, you're fairly noisy and opinionated, some people might struggle to get past you being difficult and to appreciate you as the wonderful woman you are. Therefore, get them on side before you decide to show them your warts and all – by the time they've hit the 21st exposure they'll be nuts about you anyway.

What men want

You like him

Probably most importantly, he needs to know you like him and you find him attractive.

Sexy/feminine

He wants you to look good – not necessarily supermodel-like, but to the best of your potential. He wants to feel you've made an effort for him.

Sociable

Limpets are turn-offs – he wants to be needed, but it's comforting for him to know that he's not the only appointment in your diary. Popular people make attractive girlfriends.

Prepared to commit

It's a relatively new phenomenon that women aren't as keen to commit any more. Why spoil a good thing when they have their own place, good job, great friends, good social life? He wants to feel that his partner in life wants him at the centre of her universe.

Challenging

If you're a pushover or a bimbo he'll soon tire of you. He likes a lady that has her own opinions and can make them eloquently. This doesn't mean he wants to be argued with over everything. Men hate arguing.

Supportive – gentle and kind

When he's at his most vulnerable he wants empathy, and when he's working towards something he wants your support and encouragement.

Humour

A lady who can see the funny side of life is going to make a great companion when times are great and equally when times are tough.

Trustworthy

He wants to know that you mean what you say and you're going to do as you promise.

Homemaker

Ultimately he's looking for the best genes to bring up his offspring. He wants a woman who knows how to make a home and care for the people around her.

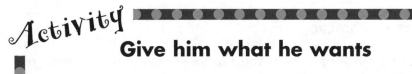

Activity Give him what he wants

- Go through each of these pointers. Do you step up to the mark on all of them?

- Prioritise them from worst to best, then work on the top two until they slip down below the next point. Switch effort to those points.

- Could some of your traits need to be tamed down until he's got to know you a bit better?

- If so what can you do to achieve this?

DATING RULES

The three phases of falling in love

When talking of love, people often refer to the 'chemistry' between them. According to recent research, during the three phases – Lust, Attraction and Attachment – there are key hormones at work. Once you appreciate these different phases, you'll be able to spot where you are in the sequence and understand the impact it's having on you.

Phase 1 – Lust

This is where you get caught up in the thrill of the chase. Outward signs of lust include flushed cheeks or neck, clammy hands and a racing heartbeat. The chemicals driving it are the sex hormones testosterone and oestrogen. Both men and women have testosterone and it's powerful stuff. It makes you want to chase after him – but resist the urge to dive for the phone.

Phase 2 – Attraction

Anything can happen here. You can loose your concentration, your appetite, your desire to sleep – all you want to do is daydream about him. In this phase neurotransmitters play a key role.

Adrenalin gets your heart racing and starts you sweating. Dopamine hits you, which is also activated by cocaine and nicotine. Finally serotonin takes its toll. In one study people in this phase were found to have 40% less serotonin than their peer group. Low serotonin is associated with anxiety and depression. If you feel like he's driving you insane, the chemical effect could well be mimicking that. However, when tested a year later, levels were found to have returned to normal.

Phase 3 – Attachment

If a relationship is going to last it must enter the attachment phase. This is important for commitment and going on to have a family. Attraction is very exciting but doesn't endure indefinitely. The two hormones responsible for this are Oxytocin, which anyone who has had a baby knows is also released during child birth and breastfeeding. It's also released during orgasm. Vasopressin is the other key chemical in the long-term commitment stage.

TOP TIP

◆ The more orgasmic sex you have, the stronger your bond will be.

Activity Identify the phases

● Think back to your previous relationships. Can you spot the duration of each of the phases in them? Did you make it through the three phases, or did you stick at phase one or two? Are you addicted to being in lust? Do you yearn for that chemical kick? You need to work harder at developing longer-term relationships and not living for the hormonal high.

● From the clues above can you spot where you are in your dating relationships at present?

DATING RULES

When should I have sex with him?

Long gone are the days of no sex before marriage. There is no cut and dried answer to this and a lot depends on your conditioning and religion. However, when it comes to finding a serious partner, the longer you can keep him at bay the better your chances for a long-term relationship.

CASE STUDY

My 8-year-old daughter asked me this very question about men the other day. My answer was, 'When you know each other very well, you're sure you love him and he loves you.' I managed to stop myself from adding, 'But you have to be over 25 and married first.' If that's the advice I give to the people I want the best for, I'd have to give the same advice to you. There are some sources that suggest that in the first 3–4 dates is average.

There is a great pressure these days to sleep with someone at the earliest opportunity – combine that with the mental desire and the hormonal urge to have sex and you've got an irresistible urge. Widespread imagery and talk of sex make casual sex socially acceptable and even expected. If you know he's not 'the one', but you've got an urge and you want to scratch it, that's a different matter.

TOP TIP

◆ Don't have sex:
  – When you're drunk
  – Without a condom
  – When you're not ready to.

Being unattainable will just add to your desirability, but be careful not to be too sexually provocative. State your position when it comes to not having sex, or he'll get mixed messages.

Another consideration is his sexual health – you don't know where he's been. You wouldn't pick a sweet up off the road and eat it so why should you be expected to sleep with someone before checking out their sexual health. More and more people these days are going hand-in-hand to the STD clinic to get checked out prior to engaging in an unprotected (i.e. without condoms) sexual relationship. If he's serious about you he'll agree if that's something you want to consider.

Activity

Are you ready to sleep with him?

● Do you know which stage you're at – lust, attraction or attachment? If it's lust, it's irresistible, but ideally wait until there is an attachment or at least a mutual attraction.

● Do you have any religious influences? If your beliefs prevent you from having sex yet, explain that to him if he's putting pressure on you. If he still won't back off, it's time to cool things off.

● Have you been conditioned into believing sex makes you wrong or dirty? Sex is perfectly natural and it makes the world go round. I know many people who struggle against this sort of conditioning. If the feeling is mutual attraction or attachment, then it's the most beautiful thing in the world. However, don't be pushed into something that you're not ready for and don't feel that you have to have sex at the first opportunity with a man as a backlash to your upbringing. See relate.org.uk for more advice.

DATING RULES

Pit stop 4 – the story so far

We're nearly on the home straight, but let's pull all the threads together, check your progress to date and make sure you're on track for a successful finale.

Flick back to Pit stop 3 (Day 55) and complete the final column.

Now we're going to consider all the elements you've learned about over the last few days and see how they relate to your dating and relationship success.

◎═ TOP TIP

♦ Complete today's activity when you're in a good mood to avoid a negative slant.

For each statement below score 2 for strongly agree, 1 for agree and 0 for disagree.

Statement	Score
My relationships at work/home are benefiting from my newly honed skills.	
I no longer find difficult people as challenging.	
I can fake confidence when I'm feeling shy.	
I'm sticking to the rules.	
The rules are making dating easier for me.	
I'm aligning my initial attitudes with 'what men want'.	
I'm more aware of what stage I'm at in the 'three stages of love'.	
I've met a guy who I think could be a Mr Right candidate.	
TOTAL	

DATING RULES

Activity

Is Mr Right just around the corner?

- How did your scores compare in pit stop 3? If you weren't already on top marks, were they improved? Did any of them drop? If so what can you do to improve them? Make a commitment to yourself to make them better.

- How did you score in pit stop 4?

11–16 You're on fire! You're taking everything on board and are going to make an entirely impressive impression on the people around you and every new person you meet. Keep up the good work – if Mr Right isn't in your arms already, he's not far away.

6–10 You're certainly going in the right direction – what is it that's stopping you from giving it 100% effort? Are you finding it difficult to adapt? Comfort zones are difficult to challenge, as are your opinions. Make the effort to embrace the remaining activities and you'll be glad you did.

0–5 You started this programme for a reason, the pursuit of Mr Right. Is this goal no longer attractive to you, or have other priorities surfaced? You owe it to yourself to take a little time each day to create opportunities and practise all these life-changing tips. For any 0 scores ask yourself why you feel like that and what you can do differently to change it. Re-read the relevant Days from Chapters 10 and 11 for advice.

DATING RULES

Your notes

CHAPTER 12

TRANSITIONING TO RELATIONSHIP SUCCESS

Make meeting his friends a success

There are a number or potentially relationship-changing moments that you need to be aware of. Depending on how you or he behave and react, they can have either a positive or a devastating effect on your relationship. As with any important event, preparation is key – you wouldn't go to a job interview without making yourself ready and anticipating every outcome. I'm not suggesting that all these key meetings will go badly, but it makes sense to eliminate as much of the risk as possible.

Starting with meeting his friends, over the next five days we'll look at how to make the best of the situation.

Their agenda

True friends have his welfare and happiness at heart. They will work to:

◆ Check to see if you measure up to their ideal of a good girlfriend for him
◆ Suss out how well they think you'll fit into their social circle.

Your agenda

You should find out:

◆ What sort of friends he has
◆ What that says about him and his tastes.

You also want to make a good impression.

Things to watch out for

◆ Leading questions or probing into your relationship history
◆ The 'bad' friend who doesn't care if they offend you
◆ Follow their lead – if other girlfriends are buying drinks, make sure you take your turn to offer.

Things to avoid

◆ Rising to the bait if you feel threatened or offended
◆ Talking too much about your relationship history
◆ Getting drunk

◆ Passing personal opinion on the suitability of his friends after meeting them.

How to react

◆ Stay calm and friendly at all times.
◆ Have some diversionary questions to use if you're put on the spot.
◆ Be interested in his friends and their relationship to him.

How to prepare

◆ Find out as much about the friends as you can from him before you meet them – particularly whether he's been out with any of them, or whether any of them fancy him.
◆ Prepare your diversionary questions: 'So how long have you known Iain for?' 'How did you guys meet originally?' 'What sort of things do you get up to together?'

TOP TIP

◆ If it's a mixed sex group, don't go dressed too sexily – if you outshine the dominant female in the group it can put you on a rocky start.
◆ If it's an all male group, go trouping the colour and be interested in all of them if you want to impress.

Activity

Meet his mates

● Think about the last time you met a boyfriends' friends. How did it go? Could it be better this time?

● Follow the guidelines above, remembering to make a stunning entrance to get you off to a good start.

● How did it go? How did your date think it went?

TRANSITIONING TO RELATIONSHIP SUCCESS

Are you keeping up? Do you need some help? If you've not already subscribed, why not try the daily text messaging service for extra encouragement and support. Just text 'Settled 81' to 80881 now.

Each set of messages costs £1.50. Please see page x for full terms and conditions.

Make meeting your friends a success

Like his friends, yours have your best interests at heart. However you don't want their over enthusiastic protection, or even out-and-out green eye, marring the prospects of your new relationship.

Their agenda

To see if:

- He's suitable for you
- He'll fit in with your social circle
- He's got any worrying secrets/traits.

Your agenda

- To make sure he gets on with them and makes a favourable impression.

Things to watch out for

- Over protective friends giving him the ninth degree
- A jealous girlfriend flirting too much with him.

Things to avoid

- Leaving him on his own at their mercy
- Him feeling like he's in the firing line
- Drinking too much.

How to react

◆ Play at being host. Field questions to him and at other friends there.
◆ Use his interests as conversation starters: 'Iain's interested in sky diving. Where did you do it, Ange?' 'Iain went travelling in the far East last year. Whereabouts were you when you went, Fran?'

How to prepare

◆ Warn him about any 'problem' friends.
◆ Warn him about any little rituals you may have.
◆ Give him a run-down on the people who will be there.
◆ Tell him any contentious subjects to avoid.

TOP TIP

◆ Speak to your most trusted friend and make sure she sits on the other side of him from you. Prime her with a couple of conversation topics and ask her to be on the lookout for any conversational hot spots.

Activity
Have him meet your mates

● Think about the last time you introduced a boyfriend to friends. How did it go? Could it be better this time?

● Follow the guidelines above – remember to get him in a good seating location to get you off to a great start.

● How did it go? How did your date think it went?

TRANSITIONING TO RELATIONSHIP SUCCESS

Make meeting his parents a success

Unless they're dead or he's not speaking to them, this day is going to come around sometime soon. It's slightly more nerve-racking than meeting your parents as it's usually on their home turf and other families have all sorts of idiosyncrasies that we're not familiar or necessarily comfortable with. To make it go with as much ease as possible do the following.

Their agenda

To see if:

- ◆ You're suitable for him
- ◆ You meet their standards
- ◆ You've got any worrying secrets/traits
- ◆ You're girlfriend or marriage material.

Your agenda

- ◆ To see what sort of family he comes from
- ◆ To see how his family communicates and interacts with each other
- ◆ To make sure you get on with them
- ◆ To create a favourable impression
- ◆ To be on your best behaviour with perfect manners!

Things to watch out for:

- ◆ His mother giving you the ninth degree
- ◆ Probing or leading questions.

Things to avoid

- ◆ Being left on your own with his mother if she's a bit protective of him
- ◆ Being too opinionated (there'll be time for that later)
- ◆ Drinking too much.

How to react

◆ Keep a pleasant tone and don't let anything take you by surprise.
◆ Use their interests as conversation starters: 'Iain tells me that you're into cooking, do you have a favourite sort?'

How to prepare

Check the following. It'll earn you brownie points in advance.

◆ Find out the family make-up. Is it a mum and dad or mum and step dad? Does he have brothers and sisters? Step siblings, etc?
◆ Ask in advance if they have any strong opinions on anything, i.e. if his mother is a fanatical vegan to your carnivorous love of veal.
◆ Find out which parent he is closer to and look to form an ally of them.
◆ If you're eating at their house, always take a gift, even if he tells you it's not necessary. A bottle of wine (if they drink) or some flowers will be fine.

Activity

Meet his parents

● Do you remember the last time you met a boyfriend's parents? Was it a success? What would you have done differently?

● Prepare yourself to make a good impression and follow the guide above.

● How did it go? Was it a success? If not, try harder next time. You may be seeing more of each other over time.

● How did they communicate and interact with each other? This will give you an idea to the sort of household he's used to coping (or not) in and, due to learned behaviour, how he may behave with you when you're living together.

TRANSITIONING TO RELATIONSHIP SUCCESS

Make meeting your parents a success

Your parents want what's best for you and sometimes they can have unrealistically high expectations. This can lead your beloved, mild-mannered mum and dad to behave in the most uncharacteristic ways. Combine this with his desire to impress them and you have a surreal situation. To try and keep the meeting as 'normal' as possible follow the guidelines below.

Their agenda

- To assess the suitability of him as your boyfriend
- To assess his potential as a husband
- If they're overly protective, to let him know he'll have to deal with them if he upsets you.

Your agenda

- For him to be shown in a favourable light
- For your parents to be shown in a favourable light
- For both parties to get on
- To have a pleasant meeting.

Things to watch out for

- Your parents interrogating him
- Your parents revealing all your embarrassing secrets
- If they're overly protective, your parents trying to catch him out
- Your parents making comparisons to your previous boyfriends.

Things to avoid

- Any of you drinking too much
- Leaving him on his own with your parents if you suspect they'll interrogate him.

How to react

- If they go off at an embarrassing tangent, bring the conversation back to a more neutral topic – one of their interests, or something they're planning.

How to prepare

◆ Tell him who will be there, their relationship to you and to each other. Warn him off topics to avoid.

◆ Give him some information on your parents interests, so he can fill in any gaps in the conversation.

◆ Tell him what would be a nice gift to bring to their home and get your mum on side.

◆ Tell your parents it's a no pressure meeting, just to be themselves and make him feel welcome.

⊙━◢ TOP TIP

◆ If your parents were particularly fond of your last boyfriend, ask them not to go on about it in front of your new chap.

Activity
Have him meet your parents

● Think back to the last time you introduced someone special to your parents. How did it go? Could it have gone differently?

● Follow the tips above for a smooth-as-can-be-expected meeting.

● How did it go? Was it a success? If so give yourself a pat on the back – although you don't need the approval of your parents, it's always good to have it. If not, was it something you did or didn't do, or are your parents impossible to please? If it's the former, try harder next time; if it's the latter, it's not a relationship breaker but it could cause friction down the line.

TRANSITIONING TO RELATIONSHIP SUCCESS

Managing work supremacy

In every relationship there is a Tarzan and a Jane. There may be times when you are more Tarzan than Jane, e.g. when Tarzan needs a little bit of support. Where the problems start is if you stay as Tarzan. You'll then have a battle of the Tarzans, which has two potential outcomes. You might have to become Jane again – if you resent this, you'll want out. Or Tarzan becomes Jane. Tarzan is unlikely to like being Jane as the whole dynamic of the relationship has changed and he doesn't like his new role in it, or seeing you living it up as Tarzan. Unless you were in a bigger job than him to start with, getting a bigger job than him may upset your Tarzan: Jane dynamic. Here's the best way to handle it to avoid upsetting your relationship.

CASE STUDY

Kevin and Mel had a whirlwind romance. They had just moved in together when Mel, despite being younger than Kevin, got a massive promotion. It transpired that Mel had been on his heels – when he'd got a new company car, she got one a couple of weeks later; when he got a promotion, she got a better one. Their idyllic relationship hit rock bottom. Mel didn't know what had happened. It was through counselling that Mel came to appreciate that it wasn't so much the promotion that had upset Kevin as the way she continually lorded it over him, making him feel inferior as a man and as a partner. She changed the way in which she dealt with news from competitive to supportive. Kevin got back to feeling like Tarzan and the relationship blossomed.

His agenda

◆ He wants to be supportive and enjoy your success.
◆ He wants to be the rock in your life.

Your agenda

◆ You want him to celebrate your success and be pleased for you.

Things to watch out for

◆ Announcing it in a way that makes him feel like he's a loser
◆ How he reacts to your announcement.

Things to avoid

◆ Making comparisons to his job progression
◆ Making him feel he should be doing more progression-wise
◆ Attacking him for not being more positive/happy about it.

How to react

◆ This is your good news – enjoy it.
◆ If he goes quiet, or defensive, tell him nicely that it's great news for you, you've worked hard for it and you want him to be happy for you. Remind him that there are going to be benefits for both of you to share.
◆ Be prepared to massage his status in the relationship: 'I wouldn't have been able to do it without your support.'

How to prepare

◆ You've got good news and you want to celebrate, but don't be upset if he doesn't see it from your perspective straight away.

Activity

Learn to tackle Tarzan

● Identify a time in a previous relationship that was a Tarzan:Jane challenging moment. How did you react to his unexpected reaction? Were you defensive, confrontational, or did you deal with it compassionately?

● Even the most wonderful man can react unpredictably at times. Be ready to follow the advice above, to keep your relationship on track and the lines of communication open.

TRANSITIONING TO RELATIONSHIP SUCCESS

Managing redundancy

It's a frightening statistic that everyone can expect to be made redundant at some stage in their working life. Although redundancy no longer carries the stigma that it once did, Relate quote it as being one of the top three reasons for the breakdown of a relationship. Knowing how to react and empathise in this situation is critical.

Their agenda

They won't have one. They'll more than likely be in shock – even if it was expected or wanted, it's still a kick in the teeth to be selected. They may try and gloss over it as something unimportant and an opportunity to try something new.

Your agenda

◆ To make sure he doesn't slip into a state of denial
◆ To make sure he knows you don't think anything less of him
◆ To make sure he knows it wont affect your relationship.

Things to watch out for

◆ Not insisting he talk if he needs some time to sort it out in his own head first
◆ Taking his resistance to talk as a rejection of you.

Things to avoid

◆ Being over-positive about the opportunities this creates – let him have some time to let it sink in and empathise with how he must be feeling
◆ Trying to rally him into immediate action – he needs to take control of the situation himself
◆ Ranting about all the things you won't be able to do now there's only your salary to rely on.

How to react

◆ Empathise, empathise, empathise.
◆ Give him some space if he wants time to process what's gone on.
◆ Reassure him it has no impact on how you view him as a man, nor on your relationship.

How to prepare

There is rarely an opportunity for preparation in these cases. He's the one who has had the bad news, so let him be the one is shock whilst you support.

Activity

Be ready to empathise

● Think of a time when you got some shocking news. How did you react? Did you immediately think and worry about how it was going to affect you? Or did you put the other person's feelings first?

● Next time somebody gives you some bad news, practise empathising. If it's a woman she is more likely to want to talk than a man. If it's a man, learn to spot the signs that he needs a chance to think about things and don't take them as a rejection of your support. Be available when he is ready to talk.

TRANSITIONING TO RELATIONSHIP SUCCESS

Your notes

CHAPTER 13

BEING A SEXUAL GODDESS

Are you a sexual goddess?

'It doesn't matter what you do in the bedroom, as long as you don't do it in the street and frighten the horses.'
Mrs Patrick Campbell, Edwardian Actress

You've found your man, you're aware of the relationship breaker situations – now it's time to move on to relationship makers. You don't have to be able to do it whilst swinging from the chandeliers to be a great lover. The shelves are lined these days with books on sex, but what it boils down to in the end is doing something that you both enjoy, at a level you're both comfortable with. Take the goddess test to check your rating in the sex stakes.

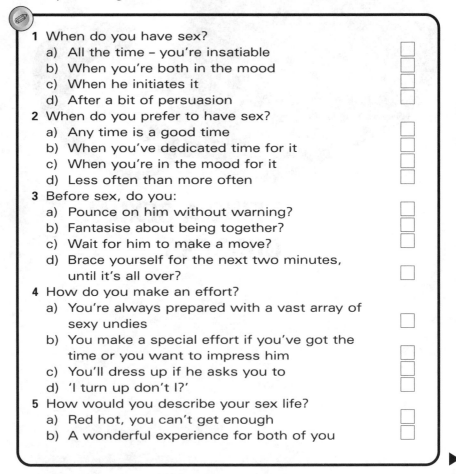

1 When do you have sex?
 a) All the time – you're insatiable ☐
 b) When you're both in the mood ☐
 c) When he initiates it ☐
 d) After a bit of persuasion ☐

2 When do you prefer to have sex?
 a) Any time is a good time ☐
 b) When you've dedicated time for it ☐
 c) When you're in the mood for it ☐
 d) Less often than more often ☐

3 Before sex, do you:
 a) Pounce on him without warning? ☐
 b) Fantasise about being together? ☐
 c) Wait for him to make a move? ☐
 d) Brace yourself for the next two minutes, until it's all over? ☐

4 How do you make an effort?
 a) You're always prepared with a vast array of sexy undies ☐
 b) You make a special effort if you've got the time or you want to impress him ☐
 c) You'll dress up if he asks you to ☐
 d) 'I turn up don't I?' ☐

5 How would you describe your sex life?
 a) Red hot, you can't get enough ☐
 b) A wonderful experience for both of you ☐

---

   c) OK ☐
   d) A necessary evil ☐
6 How adventurous are you?
   a) I've done it all, bar necrophilia. ☐
   b) We enjoy trying new experiences together. ☐
   c) I'm happy to have a go at anything he suggests. ☐
   d) We always do it in the dark. ☐

Activity
How do you rate?

Take the test and compare your scores below.

Mainly As When watching *Sex and the City*, do you see any similarities between yourself and Samantha? You're extremely highly sexed, and your sex drive takes priority over everything. Unless he's as highly sexed as you, your relationship will run into trouble. He may eventually feel like a sex slave or go off sex altogether as a protest to your sexual predator tendencies.

Mainly Bs You seem well balanced and have a healthy attitude towards sex. If you can keep the communication and sexual dialogue open you have a fabulous shot at a successful long-term relationship. Keep up the good work.

Mainly Cs Although very willing, you're not taking an active part in maintaining your sex life. Relying on him always to initiate sex and dictate the scope of your sexual relationship is storing up problems for the future. Take a more active role in initiating sex and dictating the sexual agenda from time to time – he'll be really excited that you've taken the initiative and it'll keep your relationship healthy in the longer term.

Mainly Ds Is it the man or the sex you don't like? If it's him, give him the guided tour as recommended on Day 87. You may have a low sex drive, in which case make the most of sex when you do have it. If he has a bigger sexual appetite than you this will cause problems in future – he'll think you don't want him or you'll feel used by obliging when you don't feel like it. The better sex you have, the more you want.

BEING A SEXUAL GODDESS

Learn to love your vagina

If you don't love it how can you expect him to? If you don't know how it ticks, how can you expect him to know how to send you into raptures?

It looks funny

So what, so do penises. There's no right way or wrong way for your vagina to look. Granted you wouldn't want it on the end of your nose, but it's perfectly attractive for where it's placed. Men grow up with pornography and visual stimulation. To them it's beautiful and the object of all their desires. Keeping it hidden away makes no sense at all – let them have it in full legs akimbo glory.

It smells

So what, so do penises sometimes. The French have a word for the smell which means perfume box – *cassolette*. Unless the smell has changed or you have a discharge (in which case visit your doctor) this is perfectly normal, and most men love it. They have a positive association of the smell with sex, so get used to it and learn to love it as your own unique natural sexy perfume.

It's a bit dry

Some vaginas are until they're properly aroused. It doesn't help matters if your other half is prodding away at it with dry fingers. There are a whole range of lubricants now with different flavours and textures – there's even one that heats up when you blow on it. They're great fun to play with and will keep your partner amused until your own natural juices kick in.

It's too small

All vaginas are to start with. Make sure your vagina is fully aroused before penetration and it'll grow to accommodate pretty much anything. If it's still impenetrable and causes painful spasms, you may have vaginismus, in which case seek professional help from your doctor.

It's too big

We're back to the use it or lose it tip again. Your vagina is basically a muscle – pelvic floor exercises will hone and tighten it.

I don't like to be touched there

Is it painful? Or is it because you think it's wrong? Practising yourself and working out what feels good puts you in the best position of all to teach your new man the ropes.

Activity

Get familiar with yourself

● Get yourself a hand mirror, or even better, a great big mirror. Make yourself comfy and have a really good exploration of your bits. Arm yourself with some KY and watch how it's colour and contours change as you touch yourself. It's an amazing piece of engineering. Do this regularly until you are used to seeing and touching your vagina, and enjoy its familiar appearance. Experiment in different positions to see what feels best for you.

● Set aside a quiet evening and invite your other half to a guided tour of your vagina – a strictly no penis penetration evening. Avoid alcohol as it dampens your ability to orgasm. Use whatever comes to hand (including his hands, lips and tongue) to show him how to give you a crashing orgasm. He'll be orgasmic just at the thought, never mind the actual event.

BEING A SEXUAL GODDESS

Sexual etiquette

I'm not about to re-invent the *Karma Sutra*, but what you will find helpful are some tips on sexual etiquette.

My place or his

Choose on the basis of:

◆ Where are you likely to have the most privacy?
◆ Where are you likely to be most comfortable?
◆ Where have you got the most control over setting the scene, flattering lighting, candle-lit baths, etc?

If a hotel is the best place for this then suggest to him that in order to have the perfect first time, you'd like him to arrange a special hotel room.

Pubic hair

Pubic hair used to be something that happened at puberty. Now it seems it's something to be shaved, plucked and waxed like a piece of prize topiary. These days, from a woman's perspective, less is more, although some men do enjoy a thicket of 1970s bush. I was 25 before I realised that all women had hair round their anus and 30 before I discovered men didn't expect it to be there. Porn has done the average woman a great disservice in terms of the extra work it's created in dealing with superfluous hair. Unless he's over 50, whip most of it off.

Foreskins vs circumcised

Men's lack of personal hygiene is one of the biggest factors in developing cervical cancer. Using a condom avoids this problem. However, most circumcised penises stay nice and clean with daily washing. Foreskins with enough spare skin to make a handbag require a different course of action. If you start any sexual activity with a shower or bath, it gives you ample opportunity to give it a good scrub and avoid any nasty surprises lurking in the creases. Make a point of sexily telling him this is how you like it cleaned for you to really enjoy sex.

He's useless – how do I tell him?

All women are different, hence there isn't a generic manual. Don't fake it for months – you'll get frustrated and he'll be upset when he finds out. Communication is key here. Give him the guided tour of your body and let him know what's what.

Who provides the condoms

Always carry your own – that way you know they're in date, in good condition and a type that suits you, and you won't risk having to have sex without one. In this day and age he'll think you're sensible, not easy. Make condoms more appealing by learning to put them on with your mouth (only do this with flavoured condoms to avoid a spermicidal aftertaste).

When can you stop using condoms?

When the feeling is mutually serious. You may both want to consider popping to your local STD clinic to get checked out first.

Declaring the numbers of men you've slept with

Unless he's the first, never declare how many partners you've had, or who did what best. Every man wants to be your first, only and best lover. If he pushes you on the subject say, 'It's irrelevant – you're the man of my dreams, the best lover I've ever had (even if it's not strictly true) and if I could do it all again you would be the only one.'

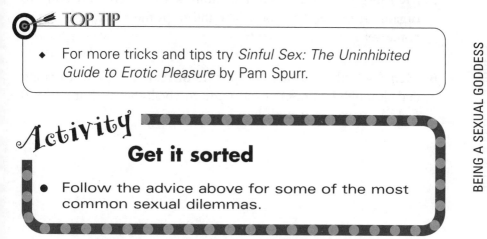

TOP TIP

◆   For more tricks and tips try *Sinful Sex: The Uninhibited Guide to Erotic Pleasure* by Pam Spurr.

Activity
Get it sorted

●   Follow the advice above for some of the most common sexual dilemmas.

BEING A SEXUAL GODDESS

10 things men want

Once you've got him trained in all the things you like, you need to take a moment to ensure he's getting what he wants.

1 Men don't like very sexually adventurous women – although men fantasise about all sorts of things, they get used to having sex their preferred way. A change is as good as a rest, but they don't want to feel outdone or overwhelmed by someone who wants to leap from the top of the wardrobe in the kumquat position whilst spanking their arse with a spatula.

2 Men love it when you're being sexy.

3 Men think cellulite is something that happens to other women. They don't care about it and don't wish to have their attention constantly drawn to it on your bottom.

4 Men don't like pillow talk. When it's all over he's quite happy to give you a cuddle and nod off to sleep – he doesn't want to talk for hours.

5 Men love it if you make it obvious when you're climaxing to orgasm. It makes their job easier and stops them asking if you've come yet at a vital moment.

6 Men don't like it when you just lie there. It takes two to tango and although he doesn't expect you to do all the work it's nice to feel like you're in it with him.

7 Men love it when you're confident about your body and forget all your problem-area hang-ups. The only bumps they notice are your breasts.

8 Men hate it when you fake orgasm, they'd rather you just said if you don't fancy sex.

9 Men love to be told they're your best lover ever.

10 Men love it when you give them even the smallest blow job. It's very difficult to disappoint them – they're just delighted to be there.

Activity

Learn what men want

● How does this compare with your preconceptions of what men want? Have you been hitting the mark? There's nothing complicated on this list – after all, men are simple creatures. To make sexual relations as smooth and as mutual pleasurable as possible, make a point of:

– Memorising it.

– Believing it.

– Doing it.

BEING A SEXUAL GODDESS

Managing rejection – dumper or dumpee ?

'Nothing happens to anybody which he is not fitted by nature to bear.' Marcus Aurelius

You'll either be skipping delightedly through the sex section with your new beau or finalising who you're going to pick from the bunch of possibles. Whatever your circumstances, even the best laid plans can unravel sometimes – you should be prepared to manage a rejection in the event that one occurs, either yours of him or vice versa.

If you dump him

When should you dump him?

- ◆ If he continually puts you down or undermines you
- ◆ If he's violent towards you
- ◆ If he regularly lets you down
- ◆ If your feelings towards him aren't mutual
- ◆ If he has totally conflicting values and goals from yours.

How should you dump him?

Either call him or arrange to meet. Explain that you've come to the conclusion that long-term you're not a good match, and it's better that you both decide to end it sooner rather than later when feelings will be even more hurt.

Don't be drawn into a protracted explanation of the reasons as he'll only get defensive and it may get heated. If he presses you for a more detailed explanation, say that your mind is made up, you wanted to tell him in person out of respect for him, but you've got to be somewhere else now. Then leave calmly or put the phone down. Do not loiter.

TOP TIP

- ◆ The key to dumping with dignity is to remain detached but respectful, regardless of whether he deserves a good tongue lashing or not. By remaining calm you stay in control and you'll feel much better as a result.

BEING A SEXUAL GODDESS

If he dumps you

Why has he dumped you?

He no longer wishes to continue the relationship. The reasons behind it are irrelevant, he has made his mind up. You may not like the method he used to dump you, but get over it.

How should you react?

Accept his decision – it takes two willing parties to have a relationship. Even if you did manage coerce him into giving it another go, he'd be off at the first opportunity and you'll have wasted valuable time that you could've spent on your next relationship.

TOP TIP

◆ The key to moving on quickly is to accept that some things are not meant to be. Getting angry with him or acting desperately won't help matters. Resolve your feelings by talking it through with friends, learning from your experiences. Apply yourself to the matter of finding a new partner.

Activity

Dumping and being dumped

● Cast your mind back to the last time you dumped someone – how did you handle it? Could it have gone better?

● Recall the last time you were dumped. How did it feel? Did you manage to stay in control of your feelings and actions?

BEING A SEXUAL GODDESS

Your notes

STRATEGIES FOR A
SUCCESSFUL
RELATIONSHIP

Are you keeping up? Do you need some help? If you've not already subscribed, why not try the daily text messaging service for extra encouragement and support. Just text 'Settled 91' to 80881 now.

Each set of messages costs £1.50. Please see page x for full terms and conditions.

Rule 1 – Sharing your hopes and dreams

We're rapidly reaching the end of the programme. In this last chapter we're putting down the building blocks of a rock-solid relationship to ensure you've made the last part of the transition from *Single to Settled*.

Once you've cracked finding a man that you're mutually attracted to, communication is the key to keeping him. Talking about each other's hopes, dreams, ambitions and thoughts creates an empathy and understanding that will carry you through each other's highs and lows throughout your relationship.

You may have talked for hours when you first met, but once you move into the attachment phase, you'll need to develop ways to resolve disputes, support at difficult times, encourage at challenges and celebrate the good times.

Ways to improve your talking and listening skills

1 Pick a good time – just the two of you, no TV, no newspapers, no phones.
2 Think about what you want to say – the topic, how it's interpreted and the response you're looking for.
3 Talk sensitively – women often talk to their partners in a way that they would never dream of doing to their boss, mother or best friend.
4 Listen and give feedback – when he's talking feed back your interpretation of what he's said to ensure you've understood. This gives him the chance to correct you before any misinterpretation arises.
5 Take responsibility for what you say – if he misinterprets don't argue over it, ensure that he understands what you are trying to tell him.
6 End the conversation – make sure you both know where you stand. By not concluding a conversation properly, he may think that you agree or disagree when you don't. If the issue is unresolved, say 'I'll think about that and we can talk about it tomorrow', or 'It's getting late, I think we should resume this conversation tomorrow.'

TOP TIP

◆ Good communication makes a relationship – poor communication breaks it.

Activity

It's good to talk

● Aim to talk frequently – little and often is better than only when a crisis demands it.

● Pick a time when you can relax together (not after sex) and discuss what you hope to achieve over the next 5 years. Ask him what he hopes to achieve too. Look for the common themes.

● Discuss a time that you spent together that you really enjoyed. Encourage him to relive the memory and input his version of events.

● Once you're very comfortable with each other, tell him about the things that you fear most and why, encouraging him to do the same.

How did it feel moving from romantic conversation to serious life-building stuff? Did the conversation flow as easily? Did you each take equal turns in talking and listening? Did you find out things you didn't know about him?

You now have some shared dreams, memories and fears. Build on these and get to know each other more intimately by talking regularly.

STRATEGIES FOR A SUCCESSFUL RELATIONSHIP

Rule 2 – Stop scoring points off him

'I'm not arguing with you, I'm telling you.' James McNeill Whistler, Artist

Arguing is a healthy and important part of communication in a relationship – where the majority of couples fall down is not being able to argue healthily.

The worst three things that you can do in an argument are:

◆ Scoring points/insults off him
◆ Setting a trap to catch him out
◆ Using violence or aggression.

7 Golden rules for healthy arguing

1 Contain the argument – don't let it last for days. Clear it up on the same day if possible.
2 Try to see things from both perspectives.
3 Do not make your partner feel inadequate, try to belittle them or be aggressive or violent towards them.
4 Don't drag up the same issues.
5 Prevent future rows by agreeing to discuss difficult topics such as where to spend Christmas.
6 Always say sorry for any hurt that you may have caused them as a consequence of arguing.
7 Forgive him for any emotional hurt he's caused you. Evaluate what went on and learn from the experience.

There is never any excuse for violence towards women – if your partner assaults you, leave immediately for a place of safety and contact the police.

TOP TIP

◆ The best outcome in any argument is a win-win situation where both of you feel you've gained something.

STRATEGIES FOR A SUCCESSFUL RELATIONSHIP

Activity

Are your arguments healthy?

Answer the questions below in relation to you and your new man. If you've not settled on one man in particular yet, apply it to your other relationships to see if they would benefit from some healthy argument rules.

1. Do your rows contain bullying or aggression?   Yes/No
2. Do your arguments drag on for days or weeks?   Yes/No
3. Do you feel he never tries to see your point of view?   Yes/No
4. Do you rarely try to see your partner's point of view?   Yes/No
5. Do you score points or belittle him?   Yes/No
6. Do your arguments go round in circles? Yes/No
7. Does it seem impossible to resolve your arguments?   Yes/No
8. Do you make assumptions about what he is feeling or thinking without checking if these assumptions are correct?   Yes/No
9. Do you hardly ever say sorry after a row?   Yes/No
10. Do one or both of you maintain long silences after a row?   Yes/No
11. Do you or he fail to appreciate the hurt that has been caused?   Yes/No

---

If you scored all 'No', you are a saint and have no need of today's lesson.

If you scored mainly 'Yes' ask your man to complete it and see if he scores the same. Work on your 'No's together. You may feel you enjoy a good argument, but your relationship and its longevity will benefit vastly from applying healthy argument rules.

STRATEGIES FOR A SUCCESSFUL RELATIONSHIP

Rule 3 – Share a little love every day

When I say love, what I'm actually referring to is affection – it's sensual rather than sexual. Just a little touch, kiss or kind word in passing, not an intentional act with the purpose of leading to sex.

The physiological benefits of being touched or receiving a kind word are immense – not only do we feel good, but it also helps to boost our immune systems. Babies not given a regular comforting touch are more likely to develop more slowly and to weigh less.

For affection to become an important and valuable part of reinforcing the state of your relationship it mustn't be used manipulatively, otherwise he'll just suspect you're after something when you're trying to be nice to him.

Don't use it:

◆ To get your own way
◆ When you don't mean it
◆ If it will cause embarrassment
◆ To make him feel sorry for you.

Affection boosters

1 Make it part of daily life. Give him a stroke on the shoulders or cheek as you pass, or a little kiss when he makes you a cup of tea or does a kind deed.
2 Use it to share in adversity. A kind word and a gentle touch when things aren't going well won't take the problem away but it will help him feel better.
3 Make time to say a face-to-face hello or goodbye and seal it with a kiss.
4 Leave a little unexpected love note. It doesn't have to be a work of massive proportions, a post-it in his wallet will do.
5 Use it to share in celebration. Letting him know how proud you are of him will go a long way towards cementing your relationship.
6 Use it to enhance a peaceful moment – gentle stroking without a word gives a sense of well-being, peace and bonding.

STRATEGIES FOR A SUCCESSFUL RELATIONSHIP

Activity
Communicate with affection

Find new ways to communicate affectionately with your man and build stronger bonds with him. Use speaking and touching affectionately to take your relationship to new emotional depths. Use the speaking tips to build even stronger relationships with your friends and family too.

Touching

1. Hold hands whenever possible. If you end up having children you'll suddenly have your hands full virtually all the time and won't be able to enjoy this unspoken affection as often.
2. Touch him in non-sexual areas, like his arms and shoulders. That way it won't be misconstrued as a sexual advance.
3. Give him a hug in passing and snuggle up in bed at night.
4. Walk touching, either holding hands or with arms slung round each other's shoulders or waists.
5. Stroke his face or hair, depending on which is his favourite.

Speaking

1. Tell him what he means to you. If you're not at the 'I love you stage', tell him how much it means to you to have him there with you.
2. Offer your support at difficult times. 'I know it's difficult for you right now, but we'll get through it together.'
3. Tell him you're proud of him. It's one of the biggest intrinsic motivators at work and has a massive impact on his self-esteem at home.
4. Celebrate the good times. 'Having you here with me today makes it even more special.'

STRATEGIES FOR A SUCCESSFUL RELATIONSHIP

Rule 4 – Make great memories to keep

The more positive events you share and enjoy as a couple, the stronger your bond will be and the more likely it is that you'll stand the test of time.

◎ TOP TIP

- ◆ Couples in long-standing relationships are more likely to stay together if they can remember what initially attracted them to their partner. Couples who can't remember early events in their relationship are less likely to remember what drew them together and more likely to bicker and split up.

Smell is one of the most evocative senses for the past. Cut grass, Christmas trees, school dinners, your mum's Sunday lunch, the smell of the dentist – all conjure up instant and vivid memories. You will both have your own natural pheromones that you've been irresistibly drawn to, but by creating scent anchors around you and the things you do together, you're cementing memories, images and feelings in his mind.

CASE STUDY

On our first holiday together, Glyn and I spent an evening in a perfumery in Palma. We tried various different scents until we picked a day-time smell and a night-time smell for me and a very sexy night-time smell for him. We had a great time sniffing all the unusual smells and bought scents that are difficult to find over here, making them even more unique to us. Every time either of us smells it on each other we go weak at the knees and instantly reminisce about the fabulous time we had together.

Choose a scent that:

- ◆ Is unique to you
- ◆ Is associated with good times
- ◆ Has a story behind it.

STRATEGIES FOR A SUCCESSFUL RELATIONSHIP

Scent anchors

◆ Scented candles from your first bath together
◆ Scented massage oil
◆ A signature flower you like to receive
◆ A sexy perfume or body lotion
◆ A sexy aftershave
◆ Fabric conditioner on your sheets.

Activity

Make some memories

Follow the points below to create happy memories.

● Take videos and photos of special events. Most phones are equipped with great technology these days – capture every moment as it happens and download it to create a virtual album. Don't forget to play it regularly together and relive those special moments.

● Develop common interests socially. Alcohol is great (I'm a big fan), but try and do something together which doesn't involve memory-clouding substances.

● Celebrate anniversaries and special days – make sure you prime him, men are notorious for forgetting such occasions. Include dates that are special to the pair of you, such as the first day you met, the first time you declared you loved each other, etc.

● Create your own unique scent anchors.

How does this task feel to you? Difficult, easy, absurd? Quite simply, it's vital for the long-term viability of your relationship – can you afford not to do it?

STRATEGIES FOR A SUCCESSFUL RELATIONSHIP

Rule 5 – Create a common 'mission statement'

Companies do this to create a common understanding of their purpose.

CASE STUDY

A company I worked for had a straightforward mission statement – 'For our product to be in 80% of automatic cars by the year 2010.' However, the actions and attitudes of the people at the company were so disparate, that rather than working towards a common goal they spent the whole time building empires until the money ran out and it became apparent that with the best will in the world it was never going to happen. Had the mission statement been 'We intend to blow £50 million by the year 2005 and not have any product in the market.' it would have been nearer the mark and they could have considered themselves entirely successful.

Relationships are no different. If you want to get married, settle down and have babies, but he wants to jack in work and travel the world picking grapes, you've got no common mission and your relationship is doomed to fail without massive compromise.

It's good to understand where each of you is coming from in order to appreciate and celebrate the achievements along the way, and to sympathise and support each other over the disappointments. Knowing how to recognise where these are without the other person having to spell it out to you is real commitment.

◎⚞ TOP TIP

A mission statement should be:
- ◆ Succinct
- ◆ Your vision for the future
- ◆ An indicator for how you want to live
- ◆ Common to both of you.

CASE STUDY

Jan passed a key exam at work. When she told Brett he matter-of-factly said, 'That's nice, well done.' Jan was really upset because she'd put her heart and soul into passing. She explained to him why she was upset and they discussed what their individual and collective goals were. Brett and Jan celebrated every achievement and disappointment together thereafter.

Brett and Jan's mission statement looked like this:

To support each other in the pursuit of each other's professional development. To equally contribute to build enough of a nest egg to buy our first home together. To respect each other and not undermine or belittle each other in anger. To give each other the space we need to pursue our own interests and to have a common interest in learning to salsa dance. To consider marriage once we've both passed all our exams.

Activity

Write your mission statements

- Write your own personal mission statement. At the start of this book it was 'To find a partner over the next 100 days'. Now that you're near the end of the programme, write one just for you. How easy did you find this? Are you very focused on what you want? Do you need to develop some more goals and ambitions for yourself?

- With your man, ask him if he was a company, what would his mission statement be? How does this compare to yours?

- Now discuss with him what a relationship mission statement would look like. How did you find this discussion? Easy, difficult, bit of a revelation?

STRATEGIES FOR A SUCCESSFUL RELATIONSHIP

Rule 6 – The relationship balance

Friends can feel very abandoned when a new man comes along – all of a sudden a chunk of their social life can go missing. Conversely, if you put your friends first and your man second, he'll feel that you're not as serious about the relationship as he is. As in all things in life, there has to be a balance.

There have been some popular writings that suggest girlfriends always come first and your man has to fit in around them. This may be the case in the initial stages of a relationship, but when you're building a long-term relationship it's coupledom suicide. As it's unlikely that you will be spending your life investing in a property and a family with friends, it makes sense to make sure that he feels the most important person in your life, but also to reassure your friends that they're still very dear to you and their support and friendship is something that you wish to invest in for a long time to come.

TOP TIP

Men don't like it when:
- You spend hours on the phone to your mother and girlfriends
- You make time for your ex
- He feels you favour everyone else over him
- You make him choose between his family and friends or you.

Four ways to make time for him

1 Cut down on the amount of TV you watch. Don't sit channel hopping if there's nothing on. Switch it off and choose some CDs to listen to together while you chat the day's events over.

2 If you have children, insist on a regular bed-time routine for them and have them in bed by the same time each night. Not only will your children enjoy the security of a routine once they're used to it, it leaves some valuable time for you and him to share a glass of wine/bath/love-making together.

3 Limit the amount of time you spend visiting your relatives or having them visiting you. If your mum's there every night when he comes home, he'll feel more like he's intruding on your family rather than you and he being a family in your own right. If you always visit your mum at the weekend it stops you from doing things together. Don't abandon your mother altogether, just explain that you've got this blossoming relationship and you want to spend more time getting to know each other to make sure he's the one. If she's reasonable she'll understand.

4 Balance your interests. It isn't vital that you go the gym every single night. Research has shown that people who exercise vigorously every day have a shorter life span! Work out between you the best times for you both to pursue your own interests.

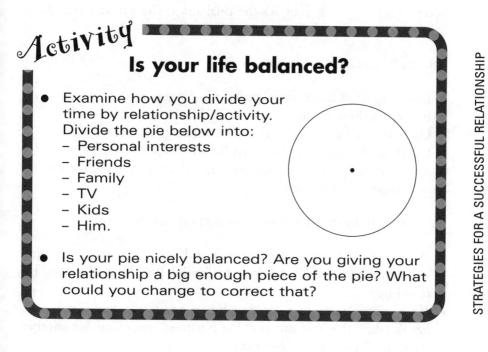

Activity

Is your life balanced?

- Examine how you divide your time by relationship/activity. Divide the pie below into:
  - Personal interests
  - Friends
  - Family
  - TV
  - Kids
  - Him.

- Is your pie nicely balanced? Are you giving your relationship a big enough piece of the pie? What could you change to correct that?

STRATEGIES FOR A SUCCESSFUL RELATIONSHIP

Rule 7 – Don't nag, learn to disattend

'All women become like their mothers. That is their tragedy. No man does, that is his.' Oscar Wilde

If you have children you will know how pointless it is to pick them up on every little thing. Eventually they cannot differentiate between what's a little thing and what's important – all requests sound the same, and in the end the parents' commands are all ignored as unimportant.

> **FACT:** Nagging is his description of your reasonable but frequent requests to do little tasks.

Men are no different. Eventually, requests to pick his towel up, put the bins out, recycle his beer bottles, pay the mortgage, take the cat to the vets, all roll into one ignorable cacophony. You're left feeling ignored and disrespected, and when he defends his lack of action by claiming you've been 'nagging' him, it's the final straw. The cyclical row about how you don't nag ensues for the nth time.

The tricks to not nagging are:

◆ Ignore most of his inaction unless it's dangerous.
◆ Ignore the little things.
◆ Do it yourself provided it doesn't encourage him to do less.
◆ Don't do it if he has agreed that he will do it.
◆ Save complaints for really serious matters only, so he will realise it's not nagging – it's serious.

How do you do this? Disattend: do nothing, say nothing.

◆ When he's run out of clean towels and has to get dried on some wet, minging thing off the floor, he'll think twice about picking his towel up.
◆ If he comes home to a stinking house covered in flies because he hasn't taken the bins out and the bin men aren't due for another week, he'll remember next time.

STRATEGIES FOR A SUCCESSFUL RELATIONSHIP

- When the cat's scratch becomes a rampant abscess and costs £300 to treat – instead of £25 for the original prescription for antibiotics – he'll make sure moggie is never left to suffer again.
- When the electricity is cut off and he can't get his report finished for work the next morning or watch his favourite footie match, you'll find all the bills transferred onto direct debit.

None of this involves nagging but it does require patience. He'll learn the boundaries of your relationship and accept fair allocation of tasks – without the need for a single cross word.

TOP TIP

- Save cross words for the really important issues.

Activity

Are you a nag?

- Think back to your last relationship. How often did rows occur due to him not doing what he was supposed to do and you nagging him? Was it every hour/day/week/month?

- If it was:
  - **Monthly** You really have nothing to worry about – nobody could accuse you of nagging.
  - **Weekly** What could you do in future to stop cyclical arguments?
  - **Daily** How much stress did that put on your relationship? Wouldn't you prefer not to be fighting every day?
  - **Hourly** Did you like this man at all? Was this a ploy to get him to leave? How much better do you feel now you're not fighting with him?

- In your new relationship, be aware that once you get past all the lust and attraction and into the attachment stage, everyday niggles will occur. Nag him and you make a rod for your own back – promise yourself you'll disattend.

STRATEGIES FOR A SUCCESSFUL RELATIONSHIP

Rule 8 – The work–life balance

'It's true hard work never killed anybody, but I figure why take the chance?' Ronald Reagan, on the reputed lightness of his working day, 1987

I take a very simple approach to work–life balance: I think of it like Mars – a little 'work, rest and play'. The quest for the perfect work–life balance has become the modern Holy Grail. Your relationship will certainly benefit if you have a good balance in your life.

Couples often make assumptions about the life they're going to have together and don't take the time to confirm that these assumptions are shared.

It may sound cynical, but there's a good chance he'll take the old-fashioned view that his job is more important than hers so she'll do all the domestic stuff, and he'll get away with just putting the bins out. She'll give him all the time he wants to play football and drink with his mates. If they have children, obviously the main burden of this will fall to her.

She may assume that there will be an equal division of labour as they both have full-time jobs, and that he won't mind her mother and friends popping round whenever they're passing.

When neither expectation is met, arguments follow.

TOP TIP

♦ Never assume – it makes an 'ass out of u and me'.

Having a mission statement deals with the big things in life (see Day 95), but to get through the everyday routine, try aligning your time, priorities and preferences.

Activity

How balanced are your days?

- Allocate your time on the chart below and answer the following questions.
  1. Do you have enough free time?
  2. Are you spending too much time at work?
  3. If there are things you'd like to do, where could you squeeze them in?
  4. Are there things you hate doing that your man could do for you, and vice versa?

- Get your man to do the same and compare your schedules. Use this as a talking point to discuss your assumptions and his. Resolve them amicably before they have a chance to develop into issues.

Work–life balance chart

Time	Mon	Tues	Wed	Thurs	Fri	Sat	Sun
6–7							
7–8							
8–9							
9–10							
10–11							
11–12							
12–13							
13–14							
14–15							
15–16							
16–17							
17–18							
18–19							
19–20							
20–21							
21–22							

STRATEGIES FOR A SUCCESSFUL RELATIONSHIP

Rule 9 – Keep your promises

There is not a more secure feeling in the world than being in love with someone you trust. Trust is fundamental in a relationship – it's often taken for granted initially, but once it's broken it's time consuming and difficult to repair. Prevention is better than cure and it's far easier to work on maintaining trust.

TOP TIP

♦ It's harder to rebuild trust than it is to maintain it.

How to maintain trust between you

♦ Don't make promises you don't intend to keep.

♦ Don't keep secrets within your relationship – but anything that happened before is your business unless you wish to share it.

♦ Keep all your promises – large and small.

♦ Don't respond with hyperbole, i.e. minimising important things, exaggerating the everyday to catastrophic proportions.

♦ Be honest but sensitive if asked for an opinion.

♦ Always behave with integrity.

♦ Don't manipulate him into doing something he feels is wrong.

♦ Express your feelings in a loving way.

♦ Always ensure you understand what you are agreeing to or promising to do.

STRATEGIES FOR A SUCCESSFUL RELATIONSHIP

How to deal with broken serious promises

It's never a nice feeling being let down, but sometimes serious breaches in trust do occur. They may seem irreparable at the time, but out of respect for your relationship consider the following points before taking radical action.

1 Don't make snap decisions – you may live to regret it.

2 Evaluate your options – they may not be black and white.

3 If you're mad, give yourself three days to absorb what's happened. This is long enough for you to process what has gone on and to calm down enough to discuss it constructively.

4 Work out **why** one of you has broken a promise – there will be a reason behind it. Finding the reason won't cure the problem but it will give you a basis for discussion and enable you to deal with the underlying issues.

5 Find the first step to restoring your trust in the relationship.

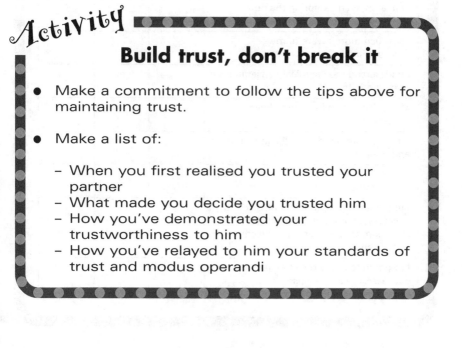

Activity

Build trust, don't break it

● Make a commitment to follow the tips above for maintaining trust.

● Make a list of:

- When you first realised you trusted your partner
- What made you decide you trusted him
- How you've demonstrated your trustworthiness to him
- How you've relayed to him your standards of trust and modus operandi

STRATEGIES FOR A SUCCESSFUL RELATIONSHIP

Good luck with Mr Right

Phew, the end! It's been a challenging few months, but I'm sure you'll agree it was well worth the effort. You've learned some fantastic techniques that can be applied with equal success in your professional and personal life. You've found some avenues to expand your social life and your mind, and best of all you've met lots of men along the way!

Activity

How far have you come?

Let's see how you're feeling now.

	Strongly agree	Agree	Disagree
I'm more confident in the way I look.			
I'm more confident in the way I feel.			
I'm more confident in the way I behave.			
I have enjoyed exploring the new avenues for meeting people.			
I'm much more aware of my surroundings.			
I understand the chemical consequences of falling in love.			
My relationships in general have improved.			
I'm more prepared for difficult situations and people.			
I appreciate more what men are looking for in women.			
I understand that attachment, sex and successful communication are the minimum requirements for a lasting relationship.			
I'm going to apply the strategies for successful relationships.			

STRATEGIES FOR A SUCCESSFUL RELATIONSHIP

If you scored all 'agree' and 'strongly agree', congratulations – you've got a great balance and a healthy outlook on relationships and yourself. Best of luck with the rest of your life, and send my best regards to Mr Right!

If you scored 'disagree' for any statement, check back to the chapters which relate to this area – this could be what's been holding you back in the lasting relationship stakes. Get back to it and Mr Right will follow!

Are you 'settled'?

Being married or under the same roof doesn't necessarily constitute settled. The way we live our lives is changing – more and more of us are choosing to live alone in our relationships. Don't feel pressured into living together or being married if it's not what you want. Being in a loving, committed relationship, with mutual support and trust is as settled as any cohabiting arrangement.

However your circumstances evolve, I wish you every success in your new relationship. If you've enjoyed the challenges in this book, don't stop here – with the skills you've developed you can do anything from progress at work to makeover your house. All you've got to do is 'Get a Life'.

STRATEGIES FOR A SUCCESSFUL RELATIONSHIP

USEFUL CONTACTS

More info on Elizabeth Clark and Rapport Unlimited
www.rapportunlimited.co.uk
www.flirtguru.com

Body Language
A. **Pease**, *Body Language* (London, Sheldon Press, 1997)
P. **Collet**, *Book of Tells* (London, Bantam, 2004)
D. **Morris**, *People Watching* (London, Vintage, 2002)

Communication
L. **Lowndes**, *How to Talk to Anyone* (London, HarperCollins, 1999)
P. **Honey**, *Problem People* (London, Chartered Institute of Personnel and Development, 2002)
The Institute of transactional analysis www.ita.org.uk

Dieting
www.edietsuk.co.uk
www.slimming-world.co.uk 0870 0754666
www.weightwatchers.co.uk 08457 123000

Free email accounts
www.msn.co.uk
www.yahoo.co.uk

Hair
www.ukhairdressers.com

Problem hair:
www.philipkingsley.co.uk
www.trichologists.org.uk

Internet dating agencies
www.dateline.co.uk
www.datingdirect.com
www.uk.match.com

Introduction agencies
The association of introduction agencies www.abia.org.uk
www.attractivepartners.co.uk
www.avenues.co.uk/
www.kno.org.uk/

Relationships
BBC Health website www.bbc.co.uk/health
British association for sexual and relationship therapy
    www.basrt.org.uk 020 8543 2707
British asscociation for counselling and psychotherapy
    www.bacp.co.uk 0870 4435252
Relate (relationship counselling) www.relate.org.uk 08451 304 016

Sex
P. Spurr, *Sinful Sex* (London, Robson Books Ltd, 2002)
T. Cox, *Hot Sex* (London, Corgi Adult, 1999)

Singles holidays
www.solitairhols.co.uk
www.solosholidays.co.uk/
www.spiceuk.com
www.twistedmartini.co.uk

Skincare
www.clinique.co.uk
www.strawberrynet.com
www.virginvie.co.uk

USEFUL CONTACTS

Problem skin:
www.skincarecampaign.org

Societies clubs & interests
Brazilian Jui Jitsu (BJJ) www.sfuk.net
Lists public speaking clubs across the UK www.the-asc.org.uk
Rileys Snooker and Pool halls www.fcsnooker.co.uk
Writers guild, for aspiring writers & details of clubs etc.
   www.writersguild.org.uk

Speed dating
www.slowdating.com
www.smartdatinguk.com
www.speeddater.co.uk
www.xdate.co.uk
www3.chemistry.co.uk

The Vagina Monologues
Tour site
www.vaginamonologues.co.uk

Video phone dating
www.dateline.co.uk/mobile Call 89799 from a mobile

Voice training
www.activepresence.co.uk